IMPATIENT FOR ETERNITY

Adam Clarke and
The Life of the World to Come

D. Gregory Van Dussen

EMETH PRESS
www.emethpress.com

IMPATIENT FOR ETERNITY: ADAM CLARKE AND THE LIFE OF THE WORLD TO COME

Printed in the United States of America on acid-free paper

ISBN 9781609472191
LCCN 2026005035

The front cover shows a 45 foot high obelisk honoring Adam Clarke at Portrush, County Antrim, Ireland. Public domain.

Endorsements

Adam Clarke was one of the most influential Methodists of the generation after Wesley. Thanks to this fine book by Greg Van Dussen we can once again benefit from Clarke's keen Scriptural insight on eternity. Here we learn not only about the life to come but how eternity is experienced in this present life, a concept central to Wesley's own theology. We also benefit from Van Dussen's own analysis and at times critique. I hope this book will be widely read and recommend it highly.

—Hal Knight, The Donald and Pearl Wright Professor Emeritus of Wesleyan Studies and E. Stanley Jones Professor Emeritus of Evangelism, Saint Paul School of Theology

The eighteenth-century Methodist divine and scholar Adam Clarke was self-taught in at least ten ancient and modern languages and knowledgeable with the corpus of Christian thought. His erudition spawned a Bible commentary still in print today. However, his linguistic work was merely a prologue to Clarke's real work: living and preaching the eternal life promised in Christian discipleship. In this volume Dr. Van Dussen, drawing on the insight of Protestant, Roman Catholic, and Orthodox theologians, explores Clarke's expansive view that for all Christians eternity begins now.

–Ronald B. Vukman University of Rochester School of Medicine

I heartily endorse and commend Greg Van Dussen's new book on Adam Clarke, *Impatient for Eternity* . It unveils aspects of Clarke and his ministry with which I was unfamiliar. A contemporary of John Wesley, I knew Clarke as the leading scholar in the Wesleyan movement of the 18th century: His massive *Commentary on the Bible* (originally published in 8 volumes) is still in use today.

Van Dussen's book prompted me to do further research. I learned that Clarke was not a sedentary scholar. Rather, he was an itinerant pastor and circuit-riding evangelist (like John Wesley), who studied while riding horseback and preached an amazing 15,000 sermons. Additionally, he served a total of seven times as president of the Wesleyan Methodist Conference in England and Ireland.

This book is focused on a particular aspect of Clarke's ministry: his views on eternity, divine judgment, hell and heaven. Van Dussen is an historian, and has thoroughly researched this theme through Clarke's writings, sermons and letters.

—Wayne McCown, Ph.D., D.D. Provost emeritus, Roberts Wesleyan University Founding Dean emeritus, Northeastern Seminary

D. Gregory Van Dussen with this work adds to his formidable series of books on early Methodist history and theology. On a personal note, if you like I am very much aware that as the Psalmist says "our days may come to seventy years or eighty...." you likely will be or should be interested in *Impatient for Eternity*: *Adam Clarke and the Life of the World to Come*. Van Dussen herein engages Clark's thought and its contribution to foundational Wesleyan theology. Greg in his usually thorough fashion and insightfulness delves into Clark's perspective on eternity and invites us to think deeply upon it. Such reflection will be a special gift for the church community and individual Christians who too often avoid the subject and thereby minimize its importance in embracing the fullness of life for which God has made provision. I highly recommend this book as a guide to reflect on what is yet before us. You won't be disappointed.

—Larry R. Baird, Retired United Methodist Minister of Upper New York

Gregory Van Dussen does not merely brilliantly interpret Adam Clarke—he channels him. *Impatient for Eternity* is both about Clarke and about Clarke speaking again, insisting that eternity is not postponed to the afterlife but erupts into the present with transfiguring power. Written with Clarke's own holy restlessness, this book embodies a theology that must be lived to be known. What once drove Clarke to preach thousands of sermons now pulses anew in Van Dussen's urgent prose. This is not historical recovery but spiritual reanimation and ecclesial revivification—Clarke's fire rekindled for a faith-starved age and a church living on processed crumbs rather than eternal bread.

—Leonard Sweet, author (*Jesus Imagination, Jesus Human, Designer Jesus*), professor, preacher, publisher, proprietor.

Dedication

To Dr. Laurence W. "Larry" Wood, Editor and Publisher of Emeth Press, with appreciation for his scholarship and for encouraging my research and writing.

Table of Contents

Foreword

From the start, Reverend Dr. D. Gregory Van Dussen draws us into a fascinating topic and serious matter regarding time and eternity by way of the great riches found in vintage Adam Clarke, the historic Methodist preacher, Bible commentator, and Chris-tian theologian. The words are so concise; the flow so inviting; the topics so engaging, and the message so clearly articulated.

Van Dussen's treatment of life and eternity begins with an expressive introduction, thus preparing the reader for a series of heart-felt matters, as appear in a sequence of chapters as follows:

Introduction

The Kingdom of God and Human Destiny

On Sanctification

On Eternity

On Death and Judgment

On Hell or Negative Eternity

On Heaven or Positive Eternity

An Adam Clarke Miscellany

Reverend Dr. D. Gregory Van Dussen is a widely experienced church leader, a nurturing mentor, and a thoughtful practical theologian, with a pastor's heart and a lifetime of effective service.

I am blessed to rummage through this latest of Greg's works. Already he's distinguished himself in extensively researched works upon other theological, biographical and devotional topics: e.g., works upon the Transfiguration of Jesus, Frontier Circuit Riders, Camp Meetings, etc.; and now, as I started to point out, this is a work drawing from the 19th century Methodist scholar, Adam Clarke, in terms of the matter of eternity.

So many analogies stand out in Van Dussen's writing which describe the human situation as a progression through life and on toward the other side of the grave. To the struggling Christian grasping to keep steady in faith although tossed back and forth by the troubles of life; to the perplexed earthling still unable, but seriously needing, to grasp the hope that there is in Christ; and to the non-committal agnostic who keeps puzzling through a worldly mire of non-commitments and misunderstandings: Van Dussen does not leave those genuinely searching abandoned, but draws upon Clarke to help bridge of the gap. Vivid, for example, is this particular nugget Dr. Van Dussen gathers:

> Far be it from God to light up such tapers to burn only for a moment in the dark night of life, and then to extinguish them forever in the damps of death. Heaven is the region where the spirits of just men made perfect live, thrive, and eternally expand their powers in the service, and to the glory of Him from whom they have derived their being.[1]

Rich in personal story and chocked full of human interest, Greg brings us back into the taproot and effective witness in vintage Methodist practice and message. As I read through his manuscript, I am thrilled by the way he gathers from the past such an expressive series of insights.

It is a message, not just given for Clarke's 19th century audience. It bears a warmth and personal good for our present-day 21st century world – a world that I believe yearns to have a rock

[1] J.B.B. Clarke, 300; 116

upon which to stand amidst present-day conflicted testimonies, great insecurities, and grave struggles that remain so prevalent.

As we turn the pages into Van Dussen's Chapter 1, "The Kingdom of God and Human Destiny," we are brought back across the years to that great affirmation of the Christian Faith, the Nicene Creed, hammered out by noteworthy leaders of the ancient church, and taught and clarified by spiritual mentors throughout the years. Right from the very start, we are told of a hope and substance in Christ for all times and places. At this point, Van Dussen springboards the heart-hungry soul from vintage Adam Clarke on to a later generation Orthodox scholar, Alexander Schmemann.

> Some people portray death as a natural and even positive part of "the circle of life." Alexander Schmemann squelches that notion. He sees it not as a mature and positive approach to a taboo subject, but rather an intellectualized escape from acknowledging and responding to the genuine horror of humanity's "last enemy." (I Corinthians 15:26, NIV) For Schmemann, death is a scourge, not to be denied or papered over, but decisively defeated and overthrown by the resurrection. Clearly this is the Biblical view and the one that offers real versus artificial hope.[2]

Thus, with a hope for our times, back to Adam Clarke, we come to what is so beautifully hard to imagine, eternity, but, with God, such a profound blessing. "When the longest period of time has passed by, it is but as a moment or indivisible point in comparison of eternity".[3]

By Chapter 2, Van Dussen draws upon Clarke's teachings regarding "Sanctification and Eternity." Citing a book title, "When Clarke Preached, People Listened," by Wesley Tracy, Van Dussen draws upon a significant insight: "Perfection is offered as our destiny by grace, not by our own achievement. Every step in the right direction gives reason for gratitude, not for boasting." Furthermore, in practical theology, as Greg points out: "Heaven is more than a far-off goal and not at all like the fantasies of popu-

---

[2] Alexander Schmemann. *O Death, Where Is Thy Sting?* Crestwood, NY: St Vladimir's Seminary, 2003.

[3] Adam Clarke, *Christian Theology,* 70

lar imagination . . . Already [it is] at the center of life for those who seek and enter it." In Luke 17:21, the kingdom of God's very being is "in your midst" / "within you."

God's design was "to restore man to his image, and raise him from the ruins of his fall; in a word, to make him perfect; to blot out all his sins, purify his soul, and fill him with holiness, so that no unholy temper, evil desire, or impure affection or passion shall either lodge or have any being within him" (Clarke's Entire Sanctification, 4-5). However, "Clarke never tries to minimize the power of sin, or to magnify humanity's ability to overcome it. Instead, it is God's grace, according to an insight drawn from Toplady, that brings the "double cure." Then, Greg points out:

> To draw near to God means discovering and living out our God-given purpose in life. We stop the forces within ourselves and our world that alienate us from ourselves and each other, and we stop living the shallow, essentially meaningless existence that passes for life.

By opening Chapter 3, one poignant sentence lays out the parameters of our earthly life: "We mortals live in a world of time and limits." However, the good news of the Gospel reaches us beyond this life and into the realm of eternity. "While there are inklings in the Old Testament, only the New Testament speaks clearly and unambiguously about eternal life and resurrection as the gateway" through which life will pass. To put it another way, Adam Clarke's theology, according to Van Dussen, is a theology of eternity and infinity.

> All time is as nothing before [God], because in the presence as in the nature of God all is eternity; therefore, nothing is long, nothing short, before him; no lapse of ages impairs his purposes, nor need he wait to find convenience to execute those purposes. And when the longest period has passed by, it is as a moment or indivisible point in comparison of eternity.[4]

In Chapter 4, by scripting some insights on Death and Judgment, Van Dussen's handling material from Adam Clarke is short, but very pungent. Take the crisp statement drawn from Clarke's

---

[4] Adam Clarke, *Christian Theology,* 69-70

Commentary: "A sinner goes to hell because he deserves it; a righteous man goes to heaven, because Christ has died for him: and communicated that grace by which his sin is pardoned and his soul made holy".[5]

From this, imagine a courtroom with a judge, prosecuting attorney, and defense attorney. The accused stands before God who holds a transcript of their lives. The redeemed, not through merits of their own, are saved through their reliance on God's grace through Jesus Christ.

Dr. Greg Van Dussen concludes this chapter with something drawn from a 19th century anthological collection published in 1880, *Last Words and Old-Time Memories*, by Ohio circuit rider, Maxwell Pierson Gaddis, which strikes me as very similar to what we of today, in this 21st century, could read as many NDE (Near Death Experience) accounts. As Greg summarizes the matter:

> In many of these stories we have bright, inspiring portrayals of the passing of faithful people from this life to the next, so that it is almost possible for us to make the journey with them. Often, they described growing light around them. Many expressed wonder and surprise at what they were experiencing, as if it were radically different from what they had expected. They were excited about all this and anxious to share their unexpected joy with those around them and others farther away. Many saw their deathbed experiences as confirmation of what they had preached all their lives. In today's skeptical and death denying culture, such accounts may be met with disbelief and explained away, but other responses are possible and conducive to hope.

In Chapter 5, Van Dussen's draw from Clarke's conception of Hell as a Negative Eternity is all of a sad, fascinating and arresting analogy, heart-felt in expression, and, yet, profound in its simplicity. How eternally sad that having given so many opportunities to repent and go God's way is the sinners' undying regret that they could have, should have chosen otherwise. Based on Jesus' story in Luke 16:19-26, Greg Van Dussen brings forth from Clarke two classic images, regarding the Rich Man and Lazarus, as "mutually exclusive mirror opposites where exquisite joy and excruciating

[5] Adam Clarke, *Commentary*, 4:83

misery exist side by side in unresolved and unresolvable tension forever." Then, among other mutually arresting passages:

> We enter into eternity: this is the unchangeable state. In that awful and indescribable infinitude of incomprehensible duration, we read of but two places or states, heaven and hell; glory and misery; endless suffering and endless enjoyment. In these two places or states, we read of but two descriptions of human beings: the saved and the lost; between whom there is that immeasurable gulf, over which no one can pass.

By Chapter 6, Van Dussen delves into Adam Clarke beautifully as he pulls out all the stops to help the reader visualize, imagine deeply, and feel heart-to-heart the great beatific vision of Heaven in terms of which Clarke has labeled Positive Eternity. For instance, Van Dussen points out:

> The overall picture [Clarke] paints is one of endless spiritual growth, learning, improvement, and enjoyment, continuing the process begun in this life, but uncomplicated by any residual sin in the self or its environment. There will be a pattern of spiritual progress like that described in II Corinthians, "from one degree of glory to another".[6] Hope will be infinite as one beautiful horizon yields to another. No reason remains for fear or anxiety since all possible causes for these will have vanished.

This 6th Chapter provides many vivid examples of how one may approach every chapter throughout Greg Van Dussen's investigation. At best, a foreword can give but a taste–a brief sketch–of what an entire book would provide, and, furthermore, it would provide a helpful welcoming into the whole book. Quite plainly Greg's actual rendering of Clarke's thoughts is chocked-full of one beautifully descriptive insight after another, expressively gathered from Clarke's deep well of Scriptural and visionary understandings.

Relishing the insights lodged in each gem, abounding in continual newness throughout eternity, Greg Van Dussen has found a goldmine in Adam Clarke for our serious appreciation, reflection, and edification, as is the joy of finding in Matthew 13:44,

---

[6] II Corinthians 3:18, ESV

among the kingdom parables, one happening upon a hidden treasure. However, the point does not stop with this. The ultimate of heaven is not heaven as being a place alone. The ultimate of/in heaven is God. Heaven would not be heaven without God.

Additionally, because of God, Adam Clarke articulates what he deems one of the finest images in the Bible as

> No cloying with the perpetual enjoyment of the same things; every moment will open a new source of pleasure, instruction, and improvement; they shall make an eternal progression into the fulness of God. And as God is infinite, so his attributes are infinite; and throughout infinity more and more of these attributes will be discovered; and the discovery of each will be a new fountain or source of pleasure and enjoyment. These sources must be opening through all eternity; and yet, through all eternity, there will still remain, in the absolute perfections of the Godhead, an infinity of them to be opened![7]

By Chapter 7, Dr. Van Dussen concludes with an Adam Clarke Miscellany, drawing out choice pieces of biographical information spanning Clarke's entire life, from childhood and youth, throughout the years, into old age. It helps to give a biographical flavor to Greg's whole treatment of Clarke on time and eternity.

"When Clarke spoke, people listened" is such an apt expression regarding Adam Clarke's experience among the people while sharing the Gospel and, accordingly, providing a sense of the respect that Clarke humbly drew.

In conclusion, Dr. Van Dussen leads us into one of the most meaningful and interesting portraits from among of the bright lights in early Irish and British Methodism, and concludes with a vignette of the respect that had endeared others to Clarke - a respect which also extended across the Atlantic Ocean into North America.

This Gospel portrait upon Eternity is truly a sensitive invitational to a life seriously lived mindful of God's call upon our lives in anticipation of eternity. As the Apostle Paul wrote to the Cor-

---

[7] A. Clarke, *Christian Theology*, 379

inthians: "I tell you, now is the time of God's favor, now is the day of salvation".[8]

—**Duane W. Priset**

[8] 2 Corinthians 6:2 NIV

Introduction

"...and shall cast them into the furnace of fire: there shall be wailing and gnashing of teeth. Then shall the righteous shine forth as the sun in the kingdom of their Father" (Matthew 13:42-43). This is a reference to DAN xii: 1-3: "Those who are wise will shine like the brightness of the heavens and those who lead many to righteousness, like the stars forever and ever."[1]

In today's radically divided world, some people, families, and groups have adopted strategies to avoid letting conversations drift into areas of potential controversy. The result can be a mutually agreed upon "cease-fire" that has the appearance of peace. The price paid for this "peace" is often a superficial level of interchange which leaves the most important things, those things people really care about, unsaid and people's deepest concerns unaddressed. The situation can be a bit like that in the height of Northern Ireland's "troubles," when some well-meaning Protestant and Catholic neighbors and co-workers tried to ignore long-standing differences and painful memories by "getting along," at least in public. The result was a veneer of civility masking their unresolved division. No one learned from each other and no understandings were reached upon which progress might be achieved. Only when strategies were implemented for deeper, more honest, but also more constructive and cooperative interaction, could real healing and reconciliation begin.

Long before these recent attempts at superficial conflict avoidance measures, there was already, in some circles, a virtual prohi-

[1] Matthew 13:42-43, Adam Clarke. *The New Testament ... Commentary and Critical Notes* .... Baltimore: John J. Harrod, 1838, III: 140; Daniel 12:3, NIV.

bition on bringing up religion and politics. The informal, unofficial ban on religious conversation put a damper on evangelism, making it harder for Christians to share the riches of their faith, outside and even inside the churches, without risking embarrassment. For many years, a variety of doctrinal and cultural factors even made conversations and cooperation between and among churches, denominations, and their constituents exceedingly difficult. In the 1960s, a program called "Living Room Dialogues" brought members of Protestant, Catholic, and Orthodox churches together for mutual understanding and fellowship and for many years, evangelical ministries like the Billy Graham Evangelistic Association and InterVarsity Christian Fellowship have brought people together across denominational lines.[2]

But the need for Christian conversation continues with the subject of this book and the writings of the early Methodist Bible scholar Adam Clarke (1760 – 1832). Clarke addressed the perennial issues of sin, death and eternal life; the dilemma, direction, and destiny of all of humanity. It seems that these topics should be of concern to every living soul. Certainly no one is exempt from their own eventual demise. As the title of rock star Jim Morrison's biography puts it, "No One Here Gets Out Alive."[3] Nor can any of us hide for very long from the deaths of others, especially those about whom we care most. The sheer weightiness of the subject prompts many to respond with humor – jokes about St. Peter at the pearly gates and the like. Others may be moved to mourn, in a limited way, the loss of a relative, friend, or public figure, and even to put forth the conviction that a good person who has endured great pain or an extended illness is "not suffering any longer;" that he or she "is in a better place now." But few will engage in serious conversation about what comes after death, the connection between flawed human nature and mortality, or about dynamics of the transition from this life to the next. An attempt to do this is likely to result either in embarrassed silence or claims to ag-

[2] William A. Greenspun, et al. *Living Room Dialogues*. Mahwah, NJ: Paulist, 1965.

[3] Jerry Hopkins and Danny Sugerman. *No One Here Gets Out Alive*. New York NY: Warner, 1995.

nosticism on the subject, the most defensive of which may hide behind a supposition that, after all, nobody really knows much about this sort of thing, do they?

Exceptions to these patterns of denial may still happen in churches; in sermons, Sunday school classes, Bible studies, and small prayer and fellowship groups, yet even here we might encounter resistance to serious studies in this area.[4]

Early Methodists across North America and beyond experienced transforming moments which brought the kingdom of heaven within reach. These moments could happen anywhere, especially in times of prayer, immersion in Scripture, and community worship. To borrow a Celtic term, these were Methodism's "thin places," where the boundary separating heaven and earth was semi-permeable and could be crossed under the right circumstances. That crossing was never something achieved by human effort, nor was it taken for granted, but always gratefully received by grace.

In these mountain top experiences, often in the context of quarterly and camp meetings, people saw, metaphorically and spiritually, heaven open and descending to earth, transforming individuals and groups, even crossing entrenched social and ethnic barriers. Fellowship deepened as obstacles to grace were shattered; people were brought closer to God and each other, and received a preview of their longed for destination in eternity. Their encounter with God and each other in some ways resembled that of Peter, James, and John at the Transfiguration, the quintessential mountain top experience. The three disciples were caught up in a mystery they could only partly understand.

In that experience, those disciples saw, without fully understanding, the glory Jesus sought to share with them.[5] There, in the immediacy of God's presence, they received his message directly.

---

[4] For a contrast, see Maxwell P. Gaddis. *Last Words and Old-Time Memories*. Cincinnati, OH: Methodist Book Concern,1880. Gaddis collected hundreds of last words and deathbed experiences of early Methodist preachers, many of them describing in detail their transition into eternity.

[5] Andreas Andeopoulos. *This is My Beloved Son: The Transfiguration of Christ*. Brewster, MA: Paraclete, 2012.

In the presence of two long dead Old Testament figures, Moses and Elijah, they saw the heavenly irrelevance of time, as well as the limited reality of earthly lifespans. All of this happened when they were away from the crowds and their familiar activities, in a dramatic, natural setting, focused entirely on the Lord.

These disciples' staggering experience came in the midst of a busy ministry. It was intended to strengthen them, and others through them, for what they were facing on the ominous road ahead. It was also designed, along with other events, especially the resurrection, to contribute to a fuller picture of exactly who Jesus is, and to authenticate his identity and purpose long into the future.[6] In a roughly similar way, early Methodists were also led away from their usual associations and activities, into dramatic, natural settings, to focus entirely on the Lord. Even when they worshiped in family or local church groupings, their transformational experiences remained intensely personal. Their time in the forest was meant to further their progress in the great salvation and equip them for challenging lives of ministry. They would deepen their awareness of, and eagerness for heaven.

A key part of what they took from these encounters was freedom from excessive or debilitating fear of death. They were strengthened with a larger and more hopeful vantage point that was far more than "wishful thinking" escapism, and given a new perspective that looked through and beyond death without denying its reality. In particular, they would still face the pain, sorrow, and loss inherent in death, but their grief would no longer be absolute. They would no longer "grieve like the rest of mankind, who have no hope."[7] They returned to their homes knowing the ground and trustworthiness of their hope.

> A genuinely Christian hope gives birth to present peace and joy. Whatever sorrows and setbacks we may go through in the short term, the long-range forecast is bright with promise. As Paul, himself no stranger to struggle and suffering, put it, "our light and momentary troubles are achieving for us an eternal glory

[6] II Peter 1:16-18

[7] I Thessalonians 4:13, NIV

that far outweighs them all."[8]

Adam Clarke, whose massive commentary on Scripture guided and informed Methodist thinking and preaching for generations and remains in print today, wrote powerfully on the theology of heaven and hell, eternity and infinity. His words can speak clearly to us even now as we seek to better understand these realities and actually "enter the kingdom of heaven." (Matthew 18:3, NIV) This is the "one hope" that transcends all others and conquers even death. (Ephesians 4:4, NIV) Clarke prayed "that heaven may be my dwelling place," in this world as well as the next.[9]

As in every other dimension of Wesleyan theology, there was for Clarke nothing automatic about heaven, nothing to be taken for granted, for "we now stand on the verge of eternity, and because it is so, now is the accepted time, and now is the day of salvation." Therefore he advised,

> Buy up those moments which others seem to throw away; steadily improve every present moment, that ye may, in some measure, regain the time ye have lost ... Time is that on which eternity depends. In time ye are to get a preparation for the kingdom of God; if you get this not in time, your ruin is inevitable; therefore buy up the time.

Given the pricelessness of the gift of eternal life, Clarke was appalled at some people's indifferent response. "How few are, in all things, living for eternity. Few are striving to excel in righteousness; and it seems to be a principle concern with many; to find how little grace they may have, and yet escape hell; how little conformity to the will of God they may have, and yet get to heaven."[10]

From an early age, Adam Clarke built his own life and ministry around his ideas of what mattered most in life and where his life was headed:

---

[8] 2 Corinthians 4:17 (NIV); Jerome Van Kuiken. *The Creed We Need: Nicene Faith for Wesleyan Witness*. N.C: Aldersgate, 2025, 71.

[9] J.B.B. Clarke, ed. *An Account of the Infancy, Religious and literary Life of Adam Clarke (etc.)*. London, UK: T.S. Clarke, 1833, 58.

[10] J.B.B. Clarke, 495-496; 370; Adam Clarke. *Christian Theology*. New York, NY: G. Lane & P.P. Sandford, 1842, 200.

> As a young preacher, consciousness of eternity did not make him "take his ease in Zion," but made him all the more active in living out his calling. Beside innumerable public exhortations, he preached in about eleven months, 568 sermons, and rode in his work many hundreds of miles. He indeed gave up his own life as lost, and felt himself continually on the verge of eternity. He endeavored to walk with God, kept up a severe watch on his heart and conduct, and gave no quarter to any thing within himself, that did not bear the stamp of holiness.[11]

His ministerial habits were very much the lot of most Methodist preachers of his day. For example, his efforts to study while...

> having to travel several miles every day; and preach, on an average, thirty days in every month, and to attend to many things that belonged to the work of a Methodist preacher. That he might [accomplish] the whole thing which he was obliged to employ in riding, he accustomed himself to read on horseback; and this he followed through the summer, and in the clear weather in general. [However, as he discovered,] The practice of reading on horseback is both dangerous, because of the accidents to which one is exposed on the road; and injurious to the sight, as the muscles of the eye are brought into an unnatural state of contraction, in order to counteract the too great brilliancy of the light. Yet what could he do, who had so much to learn, so often to preach, and was every day on horseback?[12]

Clarke's intense focus on eternity was far from an idiosyncratic quirk or obsession. His vision of eternity and its importance is a central theme in Scripture and for all of Christianity. For example, in John 6:47 we read that "whoever believes [in Jesus] has eternal life." (ESV) The present tense is noteworthy, here and in similar passages, such as John 5:24: "Whoever hears my word and believes him who sent me has eternal life. He does not come into judgment, but has passed from death to life." (ESV) While we usually think of eternity and eternal life as referring to life after death, these passages point to a continuing reality that begins in this life.

---

[11] J.B.B. Clarke,228.

[12] J.B.B. Clarke, 184.

Scripture makes it clear that restoring God's good creation is central to Jesus' purpose in the incarnation. As Charles Wesley wrote in "Hark, the Herald Angels Sing," Jesus was "born to raise the sons of earth," which points to that same centrality.[13] That raising can begin at any moment and extend forever.

Eternity is not just an endless expanse of time, but rather it stands outside of time, beyond time, interacting with time. Yet its goodness, like the One who created both time and eternity, is certainly everlasting. All of this is beyond ordinary human comprehension, but Clarke did his best to help us grasp its essential contours so that we could better appreciate the incalculable gift God offers us. Sometimes the result is clear. At others Clarke reveals his own struggles. In one of the latter he said, "Eternity is that which has no beginning, and stands in no reference to time." A more helpful effort deals with the survival of giftedness after death:

> Extaordinary talents are not given merely in reference to this world. They refer also to eternity; and shall there have their consummation, and plenitude of employ. Far be it from God to light up such tapers to burn only for a moment in the dark night of life, and then to extinguish them forever in the damps of death. Heaven is the region where the spirits of just men made perfect live, thrive, and eternally expand their powers in the service, and to the glory of Him from whom they have derived their being.[14]

Clarke also wrote about the urgency of life's decisions and commitments from the vantage point of eternity.

> Will you continue to live to the world, and forget that you owe your being to God, and have immortal souls which must spend an eternity in heaven or hell, according to the state they are found in when they leave this world? We have no time to spare, scarcely to deliberate in: the judge is at the door, and death is not far behind. I have tried both lives; and find that a religious life has an infinite preference beyond the other.[15]

---

[13] Charles Wesley, "Hark, the Herald Angels Sing," Our Great Redeemer's Praise. Franklin,TN: Seedbed, 2022, 180, v. 3.

[14] J.B.B. Clarke, 300; 116.

[15] J.B.B. Clarke, 182.

The perspective of eternity is actually the best way to deal with the often perplexing character of life in this world, even when Scripture and faith seem to be the source of our perplexity. Once when Jesus' disciples were confused by his words and some less committed among them turned away, Jesus asked his inner circle if they would also be leaving. But Peter replied for them all when he said, "Lord, to whom shall we go? You have the words of eternal life, and we have believed, and have come to know, that you are the Holy One of God. (John 6:68-69, ESV.) Peter may well have been as perplexed as those who were leaving, but he trusted Jesus and his "words of eternal life," and for the time, that was enough. Peter did not have to know everything when he knew the most important thing.

Chapter 1

Adam Clarke on the Kingdom of God And Human Destiny

"'For God so loved the world, that he gave his only begotten Son, that whosoever believeth in him should not perish, but have everlasting life.' Such a love as that which induced God to give his only begotten Son to die for the world, could not be described:- Jesus Christ does not attempt it."[1]

I have been blessed with several opportunities to celebrate, together with Catholic priests, the weddings of Catholic/Methodist couples. On one of these occasions, we included the Nicene Creed as part of the ceremony. Afterwards, at the reception, one of the guests, who was clearly moved by that inclusion, came up to me and said, "You have no idea how much that meant to us!" When I asked what he meant, he replied, "There we were, more than three hundred people from different churches, all saying we believe these same things!" While doctrinal and practical differences remained, in that moment unity was more important, certainly to the newly married couple, but also to at least one guest who had vowed to uphold them in their marriage.

Various authors have written on the importance of the Creed, often for the unity it expresses. It provides a reminder and clarification of central Christian beliefs; an affirmation of historic, communal identity. It offers a way of saying publicly, "this is where we stand." Luke Timothy Johnson says that the Creed "communicates a compelling vision of the world's destiny and humanity's role that challenges the accustomed idolatries and the weary

[1] Adam Clarke, *Commentary*, Baltimore, MD: John J. Harrod, 1838, 536.

platitudes of current worldly wisdom. Christians who say these words ... [are] celebrating a specifically Christian conception of reality...."[2] We need this oft-repeated reminder of teachings that are too easily forgotten or may have grown murky with the passing of time.

The Nicene Creed understandably took time to achieve universal consensus. For a time there were many local creeds that sought to make necessary adjustments or affirm the orthodoxy of a particular bishop. One of the latter was the creed of St. Patrick in Ireland, included in his *Confession* or spiritual autobiography, which shows the influence of Nicaea, as well as Scripture:

> For there is not, nor ever was, any other God - there was never before him and there shall not be any after him (Cf. Isaiah 43:10-11) - besides him who is God the Father unbegotten: without a source, from him everything else takes its beginning. He is, as we say, the one who keeps hold of all things. (Cf. Colossians 1:17)
>
> And his Son, Jesus Christ, whom we profess to have always existed with the Father. He was spiritually with the Father before the world came into being; begotten of the Father the beginning of anything in a way that is beyond our speech. And through him all things were made, all things visible and invisible. (Cf. John 1:3; Colossians 1:16) He was made man, and having conquered death was taken back into the heavens to the Father. (Mark 16:19) 'And [the Father] has bestowed on him all power above every name in heaven and on earth and under the earth, so that every tongue may confess that [our] Lord and God is Jesus Christ' (Philippians 2:5-11) in whom we believe. And we look forward to his coming, in the time that is soon to be, when he will be the judge of the living and the dead, 'who will repay each one according to his works.' (Romans 2:6)
>
> And '[the Father] has plentifully poured upon us the Holy Spirit', (Titus 3: 5-6) and the gift and pledge of immortality, who makes those who believe and listen into 'sons of God' the Father 'and fellow heirs with Christ.' (Cf. Romans 8: 14-19) [This is] who we

[2] Luke Timothy Johnson. *The Creed: What Christians Believe and Why It Matters*. New York, NY, et al: Doubleday, 2003, 7.

confess and adore, One God in Trinity of sacred name.[3]

The conclusion of Nicaea, further clarified by subsequent councils, proved to be an anchor for the Church amid stormy ecclesiastical seas; an anchor also for storm-tossed souls trying to navigate the tempests of life. The Creed, and the faith to which it testifies, offers much needed stability and strength to God's people. As Adam Clarke would one day write regarding one vital affirmation of the Creed:

> The hope of eternal life is represented as the soul's anchor; the world is the boisterous, dangerous sea; the Christian course the voyage; the port everlasting felicity; and the veil, or inner road, the royal dock in which that anchor was cast. The storms of life continue but a short time. The anchor, hope, if fixed by faith in the external world, will infallibly prevent all shipwreck; the soul may be variously tossed by various temptations, but will not drive, because the anchor is in sure ground, and itself is steadfast; it does not drag, and it does not break; faith, like the cable, is the connecting medium between the ship and the anchor, or the soul and its hope of heaven; faith sees the haven, hope desires and anticipates the rest; faith works, and hope holds fast; and shortly the soul enters into the haven of eternal repose.[4]

Here we have just one - though an important one - reason to rejoice.

> In the end, those who championed the teaching and language of Nicaea prevailed. Figures such as Athanasius, Basil the Great, Hilary of Poitiers, and Gregory of Nazianzus, among many others, played crucial roles in helping the Church explain and defend "the faith which was once for all delivered to the saints" (Jude 3) The years of controversy were not wasted; the Church attained greater clarity about its own confession of the divine Trinity (the Father, Son, and Holy Spirit).[5]

---

[3] Jared Ortiz and Daniel A. Keating. *The Nicene Creed: a Scriptural, Historical, and Theological Commentary*. Grand Rapids, MI: Baker Academic, 2024, 9; Thomas O'Loughlin. *Discovering Saint Patrick*. Mahwah, NJ: Paulist, 2005,144-145.

[4] Adam Clarke. *Christian Theology*. New York, NY: G. Lane & P.P. Sand- ford, 1842,180-181.

[5] Ortiz & Keating, *Nicene Creed*, 8.

Far from being an arcane, obsolete case of semantics enshrined in ritual,

> ...It guards, describes, and expresses forever the very essence of Christianity, the joyous mystery of the Gospel. God is united with man, but in that union man is preserved in all his fullness; he is in no way diminished. ... What might seem outwardly a mere rhetorical balance of words expressed in fact the faith, hope, and love of the Church, the moving force of all our Christian life.[6]

When we focus on human destiny, whether for a single person or all of humanity, the last two lines of the Nicene Creed are especially compelling. They commonly read,

> We look for the resurrection of the dead,
>
> and the life of the world to come. Amen.

This is how they appear in many versions, including the Global and United Methodist Churches'. To these lines we could well add this one, which appears earlier:

> and his kingdom will have no end.
>
> This line reflects a key characteristic of the "life of the world to come" – its eternality.

The current Catholic rendering makes two changes:

> I look forward to the resurrection of the dead
>
> And the life of the world to come.

Putting the first line in the first person singular loses some of the communal emphasis of the plural without altering the meaning. Looking "*forward* to the resurrection" emphasizes the positive, hopeful sense of longing for what has been promised, without changing its content. Johnson points out that this hopeful sense actually translates the Greek word for "expect," which justifies the addition. Johnson spells out the nature of Christian expectation:

---

[6] Alexander Schmemann. *The Historical Road of Eastern Orthodoxy*. Crestwood, NY: St. Vladimir's Seminary, 1977, 136.)

> We hope that as embodied creatures, and as God's people, we shall in the end reach the full sharing in God's own life that Jesus, "the pioneer and perfecter of faith," has achieved (Heb 12:2), that we might find full conformity to the body of Christ. As Paul says, "Our citizenship is in heaven, and it is from there that we are expecting a Savior, the Lord Jesus Christ. He will transform the body of our humiliation, that it might be conformed to the body of his glory, by the power that also enables him to make all things subject to himself" (Phil 3:20-21).[7]

As a child, when I started thinking and reflecting on eternity, it was the flip side of a common, understandable fear of death and dying. A lot can be learned from the right kind of meditation on mortality, such as this reflection on earthly glory by Adam Clarke after visiting Winchester Cathedral in 1786:

> How little is worldly grandeur worth, together with all the most splendid distinctions, which great and pompous titles, or even important offices, confer upon men! They vanish as a dissipated vapour, and the proprietors of them go their way; and where are they? or of what account? Death is the common lot of all men: and the honours of the great, and the abjectness of the mean, are equally unseen in the tomb. This I saw abundantly exemplified to-day, while viewing the remains of several kings, Saxon and English, whose very names, much less their persons and importance, are scarcely collectible from 'Rosy damps, mouldy shrines, dust, and cobwebs.' This exhibits a proper estimate of human glory.... The meanest living slave is preferable to all these dead potentates. Is there any true greatness, but that of the soul? And has the soul any true nobility unless it is begotten from above, and has the spirit and love of Christ to actuate it? surely none. The title of Servant of the Lord Jesus, I prefer to the glory of these kings: this will stand me in stead, when the other, with all its importance, is eternally forgotten.[8]

Some people portray death as a natural and even positive part of "the circle of life." Alexander Schmemann squelches that notion. He sees it not as a mature and positive approach to a taboo

---

[7] Johnson, 285;

[8] J.B.B. Clarke, ed. *An Account of the Infancy, Religious and Literary Life of Adam Clarke* (ETC.). New York, NY: Appleton, 1833, 194.

subject, but rather an intellectualized escape from acknowledging and responding to the genuine horror of humanity's "last enemy." (I Corinthians 15:26, NIV) For Schmemann, death is a scourge, not to be denied or papered over, but decisively defeated and overthrown by the resurrection. Clearly this is the Biblical view and the one that offers real versus artificial hope.[9]

Of greater importance are meditations on the resurrection.

> On the third day, Christ rose again – not in metaphor, not in memory, but in **bodily reality**. The tomb was empty. The linen cloths were set aside. He appeared to the disciples, to the myrhh-bearing women, to Thomas, and to over five hundred brethren. His resurrection is not the reversal of death, but its **destruction**. ... The Resurrection is the vindication of Christ's identity, the seal of our hope, and the pledge of the age to come. ... In the risen Christ, human nature is glorified, the body is transfigured, and mortality is clothed in incorruption.[10]

Nectarios takes his point from Paul's First Letter to the Church at Corinth:

> "So will it be with the resurrection of the dead. The body that is sown is perishable. It is raised imperishable; it is sown in dishonor, it is raised in glory; it is sown in weakness, it is raised in power; it is sown a natural body, it is raised a spiritual body."[11]

Thus the last lines of the Nicene Creed are far from inconsequential. Instead they make ultimate sense out of universal calamity.

> The Creed ends with the end, and with our Christian hope that this life is not all there is and that death is not the final word. Based on our belief in all the previous articles of the Creed, we can look forward with hope (for hope is faith directed toward the future) to a life with God that includes not only our soul but our body. The Creed does not go into great detail about this future; it gives us only the barest, though most essential, outline of what

---

[9] Alexander Schmemann. *O Death, Where Is Thy Sting?* Crestwood, NY: St Vladimir's Seminary, 2003.

[10] Chorbishop Nectarios. *The Faith Once Delivered: A Case Introduction to Orthodox Theology*. N.C.: St. Stephen' Media, 2025, section 7.5, n.p.

[11] I Corinthians 15:42-44, NIV

believers can hope for.[12]

The Book of Ecclesiastes describes the limits of human wisdom about the course of life and death; the emptiness and futility of life that is limited to this world. But the author also writes of eternity and hope, saying that God "has set eternity in the human heart." This is made evident in the heavenly values that resonate within us, in spite of our confusion and corruption.[13]

There are many aspects of everyday life that point to and ultimately derive from eternity. They include ordinary things we value that are powerful, abiding, steadfast, and lasting, like real wool Oriental carpeting, carefully crafted hardwood furniture (I especially appreciate quarter sawn oak furniture originating with the Roycroft Community in East Aurora, New York; Koa furniture in Hawaii) and clothing (like Donegal and Harris Tweeds from Ireland and Scotland) or things in nature, like mountains, or the precious stones and metals they contain, or old-growth trees. These same qualities are among those we most cherish and admire in God. Words like solid, strong, reliable, durable, timeless, permanent, unshakable, deep, immovable, profound, unbreakable, as opposed to transitory, flimsy, temporary, shallow, weak, shaky, unreliable, superficial, frail, breakable, fragile. Most of the time we naturally prefer things that are sturdy, things that endure, rather than their opposites. The same is true with people and relationships: we tend to prefer someone who is trustworthy over someone we cannot depend on. We applaud business ventures that survive competition and the uncertainties of the marketplace. There is a pizza shop in the town where I live that boasts of its longevity: "since 1947," making it the oldest pizzeria in town. Come to think of it, that's my age, too! We celebrate lasting marriages, and even when they don't last, or shouldn't last, because they're built on shaky foundations; even when they topple before powerful storms, "forever" remains our goal, the hope we start out with, even the second time around. Travelers to Europe are invariably impressed by the age of churches, castles, and

[12] Ortiz & Keating, *Nicene Creed*, 199.

[13] Ecclesiastes 3:11 NIV

ancient monuments like Newgrange or Stonehenge because they have survived the ravages of time and retain their magnificence. The same fascination draws visitors to the pyramids of Egypt and the Great Wall of China.

But eternity is far more than survival across time. "The life we receive in the resurrection will not be more of this life, but a new, transformed, and glorified life – what the New Testament calls 'eternal life' (e.g. John 5:24)."[14]

Eternity adds the dimension of depth and profound meaning, and just as we mortals can experience endurance and strength in this life, giving us limited tastes of the permanence of heaven, we can also receive what David Adam has called "glimpses of glory" in revelations from the heart of God's kingdom.[15]

My early intimations of eternity occurred in in-depth conversations, friendships, and fellowship during my college years and thereafter. Many of these experiences were strengthened by music, whether in concerts, worship, or group singing. Some of these were very personal and also deeply intellectual conversations with the girl who is now my wife. One was a campfire at Wasaga Beach, Ontario, on the Georgian Bay, where my wife and I were invited into a circle of strangers from Toronto that quickly developed into an intense friendship. Another came on a retreat with college students where the fellowship led me to write a song that recognized the divine Source and connection that would continue all through my life:

"On this Day" (DGV)

Everything that I am

Has come with me today;

Every place that I've been

Passing through along the way:

I offer up my whole life now

---

[14] Ortiz & Keating, *Nicene Creed*. 200.

[15] David Adam. *Glimpses of Glory*. SPCK, 2000.

To my Lord, our Lord on this day.

All the friends I've ever known

Are part of me today

And all your creation

Has moved me to this day:

I offer up my whole life now

To my Lord, our Lord on this day.

The changes I have lived through

Are grounded in your love;

The vision that I see now

Is what I've seen in love:

I offer up my whole life now

To my Lord, our Lord on this day.

Sometimes I consciously sought God in those encounters; at other times the eternal dimension began as an unexpected mystery. Always there was a greater depth to the moment than had been there before, which, sooner or later I/we recognized as the presence of God and the kingdom of heaven. Those moments were often long-remembered and always received with joy and gratitude.

How do we recognize experiences like these as eternal? One necessary marker surely is love, which after all is the essential character of God and his kingdom. Love abides in the heart of God. Love is reflected in our lives increasingly as his new creation grows in us. Love binds us together as we open ourselves to the Source of love. Love is not the fleeting, unreliable thing its counterfeits are, so that dependability is itself a sign of the eternal. Adam Clarke wrote:

> "God is love:" [I John 4:8] and in this an infinity of breadth, length, depth, and height is included; or rather all breadth, length, depth, and height are lost in this immensity. It comprehends all that is above, all that is below, all that is present, all that is past, and all that is to come. In reference to human beings, the love of God in its breadth is a girdle that encompasses the globe, or a mantle in which it is wrapped up. Its length from the eternal purpose of the mission of Christ, to the eternity of blessedness which is to be enjoyed by the pure in heart in his ineffable glories. Its depth reaches to the lowest-fallen of the sons of Adam, and to the deepest depravity of the human heart; and its height to the infinite dignities of the throne of Christ.[16]

Clarke explains further the central, foundational place of love among "all other graces" in human life:

> Love is the means of preserving all other graces; indeed, properly speaking, it includes them all; and all receive their perfection from it. Love to God and man can never be dispensed with. It is essential to social and religious life; Without it no communion can be kept up with God; nor can any man have a preparation for eternal glory whose heart and soul are not deeply imbued with it. Without it there never was true religion; nor ever can be; and it not only is necessary through life, but will exist throughout eternity. What were a state of blessedness if it did not comprehend love to God and to human spirits in the most exquisite, refined, and perfect degrees?
>
> That man is no Christian who is solicitous for his own happiness alone, and who cares not how the world goes, so that himself be comfortable. How much good is omitted, how many evils caused, how many duties neglected, how many innocent persons deserted, how many truths suppressed, and how many acts of injustice authorized, by those timorous forecasts of what may happen, and those faithless apprehensions concerning the future![17]

Another sign is the way eternity lifts us beyond ourselves toward God and others and out of preoccupation with ourselves. While it builds us up, that building up is not at the expense of

[16] Adam Clarke, *Christian Theology*,75-76.

[17] A. Clarke, *Christian Theology*, 168.

others; it is seen in the humility and generosity it engenders. An eternal perspective may enhance our attractiveness, but in a way that is translucent. The light of Christ shines through us, so that his light, not our personality, is the ultimate attraction. In this way "the light of the world" (Christ) becomes "the light of the world (in his disciples)."[18]

Eternity becomes the Christian's destination and present reality. "The resurrection of the dead is the central hope of the Christian life. ... Without hope for our own bodily resurrection, there is no Christianity."[19]

In I Corinthians 15, Paul takes great pains to show just how much is at stake in the teaching of the resurrection and the reality behind it. He says the message of Jesus' triumph over death is "of first importance" among teachings passed on by the Church, and that the resurrection itself was supported by the testimony of more than five hundred eyewitnesses. He says that, "if Christ has not been raised, our preaching is useless and so is your faith." Every shred of credibility is gone from the Christian proclamation unless its factual, historical substance is actually true. The futility of a false proclamation is pathetically clear: "If only for this life we have hope in Christ, we are of all people most to be pitied." But Paul and his resurrection message are rock solid, completely reliable, and so he can brush all doubts aside, saying, Christ has indeed been raised from the dead." And this essential reality is the foundation of many more blessings, for Christ is not risen alone, but is "the firstfruits of those who have fallen asleep." There is a way for us to get beyond "the last enemy," which is death and which will be finally and forever crushed, subjugated and disempowered by God. Paul continues with his contrasts between futility and triumph, including his own experience: "If I fought wild beasts in Ephesus with no more than human hopes, what have I gained?" But in fact, "Death hs been swallowed up in victory."[20]

Eternity shapes our values and priorities, helping us sort out the things that matter from those that do not. Among the things

---

[18] John 8:12; Matthew 5:14.

[19] Ortiz & Keating, *Nicene Creed*, 201.

[20] I Corinthians 15:3; 5-8; 14; 19-20; 26; 32; 54, NIV

that do matter, eternity enables us to choose what matters most, what best fulfills our gifts and calling, and serves the greatest need, all the while drawing us closer to God.

> All time is as nothing before him, because in the presence as in the nature of God all is eternity; therefore nothing is long, nothing short before him; no lapse of ages impairs his purposes, nor need he wait to find convenience to execute those purposes. And when the longest period of time has passed by, it is but as a moment or indivisible point in comparison of eternity.[21]

There is a strong link between eternity and inspiration. In a moment of inspiration, there is a breakthrough into our world from God's kingdom, one that brings extraordinary insight, wisdom, creative impulse, energy, and love. Inspired people offer the world exceptional talent, compassion, vision, discernment, beauty, and purpose. Inspiration can be explicitly sacred or secular. In the latter category, the inspired person may be unaware of the inspiration and especially of its heavenly, eternal origin. That person may not realize that anything special has happened, or if they do realize its specialness, they might be content to take credit themselves.

An example of apparently secular inspiration that I would give comes in the form of two ballads by the Canadian folksinger Gordon Lightfoot. They are "The Canadian Railroad Trilogy" and "The Wreck of the Edmund Fitzgerald." Both are rooted in history, the first covering grand sweeping vistas of time and hard won progress, the other narrowly focused on a single disaster. Both songs can generate powerful emotions, supported by moving instrumental backgrounds. There is nothing particularly religious about these songs, although The Edmund Fitzgerald mentions the church where the dead sailors were memorialized and raises the classic problem of evil by questioning why such tragedies are permitted by an apparently unconcerned or uninvolved God. Yet in spite of their secular nature, several marks of inspiration remain: compassion, beauty, insight, and creativity are all present.

[21] Adam Clarke, *Christian Theology*, 70.

Whether technically inspired or not, surely they are gifts to be appreciated.

The nature of eternity also reminds us that "God dwells with his people forever. (Romans 8:18-25; II Peter 3:13; Revelation 21-22) ... Personhood is permanent - Neither death itself nor *nirvana* afterwards spells the end of your distinctive self."[22] There is continuity in the person you are that extends across the panorama of time and eternity, which makes it of utmost importance, not only the discrete thoughts and actions of particular moments, but the character of the person which they express and to which they contribute. It is the trajectory of a person's life that matters most.

Adam Clarke approached eternity in the right spirit, a spirit of humility.

> "O, may I to eternity lie in deep humility at His feet, recognizing the immenseness of His mercy, and the utter utter unworthiness of the subject on which it has wrought so many miracles, truly expressive of its own unconfined benignity!" [That same graciousness can be known in this life as well as in the life to come:] "Do you wish to know how I was taken care of during my illness? I indeed lacked nothing that could be procured; nor was there any difficulty to procure persons to sit up with me day or night.... May the good Lord to eternity reward them for what they have done for His unworthy servant."[23]

He described another trait of someone who was fixed on eternity, an older woman who to him embodied "all the solemnity and majesty of Christianity" summarized in the single word "ETERNITY, in that importance in which it is considered by those whose minds are devoted to deep reflection." Both humility and "solemnity" are grounded in "the *eternal unoriginated nature* of Jesus Christ," reflected in transformed humanity.[24]

Clarke's philosophical descriptions of Christ are rooted in the Nicene Creed and the theology behind it. Thus he said, "His *Divine Nature* [as distinct from his human nature], because God,

---

[22] Jerome Van Kuiken, *The Creed We Need: Nicene Faith for Wesleyan Witness.* N.C: Aldersgate, 2025, 67-68.

[23] J.B.B. Clarke, 306-307.

[24] J.B.B. Clarke, 302; 93.

infinite and eternal, is uncreated, underived, and unbegotten."[25] He continually stressed the changelessness of "Almighty and everlasting God" and eternity, saying, "...there is but one uncreated, unoriginated, infinite, and eternal Being; the Creator, Preserver, and Governor of all things.

> *Repentance*, faith, and holiness are unchangeable in their nature, and uniform in their effects. Religion has to do with one God, one Mediator, one Sacrifice; it recommends one faith, enjoins one baptism, proclaims one heaven, and one hell. All these are unchangeable both in their nature and their effects. One Gospel is the fountain whence all these things are derived; and that Gospel being the everlasting Gospel, was, is, and will be the same, from its first publication, till time shall be no more." (259; 172; 79.)

These references may well remind us of the Letter of James' comment about "the Father of heavenly lights, who does not change like shifting shadows," (James 1:17, NIV) and also the unity produced by love, so powerfully put forward by Paul in Ephesians. Note the connection between love, humility, and oneness in Paul's Letter:

> Be completely humble and gentle; be patient, bearing with one another in love. Make every effort to keep the unity of the Spirit in the bond of peace. There is one body and one Spirit, just as you were called to one hope when you were called; one Lord, one faith, one baptism; one God and Father of all, who is over all and through all and in all.[26]

This picture of unity is meant to inspire God's people to a way of life that reflects and builds toward his eternal kingdom, a kingdom of "infinite wisdom and love," characterized by "infinite purity and justice," planned and coordinated by the "infinite mind" of the One who has revealed himself as the "Infinite, eternal I AM."[27]

---

[25] J.B.B. Clarke, 173.
[26] Ephesians 4:2-6, NIV.
[27] J.B.B. Clarke, 173; 214; 94; 107; 299.

Chapter 2

Adam Clarke on Sanctification and Eternity

"May God himself, the God of peace, sanctify you through and through. May your whole spirit, soul and body be kept blameless at the coming of our Lord Jesus Christ. The one who calls you is faithful, and he will do it." (I Thessalonians 5: 23-24, NIV).

"May he sanctify you to the end, and to the uttermost; that, as sin hath reigned unto death, even so may grace reign through righteousness unto eternal life by Jesus Christ our Lord.[1]

Interpreting Acts 1:5, Clarke said: "John baptized with water, which was a sign of penitence, in reference to the remission of sin; but Christ baptizes with the Holy Spirit, for the destruction of sin [i. e., entire sanctification]."[2]

Holiness is lifted up as an ideal, however rare, in the fifteenth Psalm. Its description of the person who is qualified to stand and worship in God's presence suggests the characteristics of those who are preparing for heaven:

> Who may worship in your sanctuary, Lord?
> Who may enter your presence on your holy hill?
> Those who lead blameless lives and do what is right,
> Speaking the truth from sincere hearts.
> Those who refuse to gossip
> or harm their neighbors
> or speak evil of their friends.
> Those who despise flagrant sinners,
> and honor the faithful followers of the Lord,
> and keep their promises even when it hurts.
> Those who lend money without charging interest,

[1] Adam Clarke, *Commentary*, IV; 572.
[2] Adam Clarke, *Commentary*, V; 683.

> and who cannot be bribed to lie about the innocent.
> Such people will stand firm forever. (Psalm 15, NLT)

Of all the topics in Clarkes sermons, "holiness was his most stressed subject...."[3] The realization of the perfection of eternity should not cause us imperfect mortals discouragement or despair. Perfection is offered as our destiny by grace, not by our own achievement. Every step in the right direction gives reason for gratitude, not for boasting. "Had he [Christ] not been incarnated, suffered, and died in our stead, we could not receive either pardon or holiness; and did he not cleanse and purify our hearts, we could not enter into the place where all is purity...."[4]

Clarke goes on to explain,

> This perfection is the restoration of man to the state of holiness from which he fell, by creating him anew in Christ Jesus, and restoring to him that image and likeness of God which he had lost.
> ...
>
> The whole design of God was to restore man to his image, and raise him from the ruins of his fall; in a word, to make him perfect; to blot out all his sins, purify his soul , and fill him with holiness, so that no unholy temper, evil desire, or impure affection or passion shall either lodge or have any being within him; this and this only is true religion or Christian perfection; and a less salvation than this would be dishonorable to the sacrifice of Christ, and the operation of the Holy Ghost; and would be as unworthy of the appellation of Christianity....[5]

In pursuing this perfection in Christ, we seek nothing less than the blessing of becoming "like him." (I John 3:2, NIV) Were this undertaken as a matter of proud ambition, as if we could manufacture it within ourselves, such a pursuit would be impossible and ridiculous. But as a promise of the Holy Spirit it becomes an entirely different matter. Paul wrote to the Corinthians that "we ... are being transformed into his image with ever-increasing

---

[3] Wesley Tracy. *When Adam Clarke Preached, People Listened.* Kansas City, MO: Beacon Hill, 1981, 45.

[4] Adam Clarke. *Entire Sanctification.* N.C.: Dekton, 2022, orig.1874, 2.

[5] Adam Clarke, *Entire Sanctification*, 4-5.

glory, which comes from the Lord, who is the Spirit. (II Corinthians 3:18, NIV) We do not shape ourselves into his image, but we have the opportunity to be shaped in that way by God's gracious action. All we can do is cooperate, making ourselves available for a grace-initiated *synergeia*. Hence Paul's charge to Timothy: "take hold of the eternal life to which you were called.... (I Timothy 6:12, NIV; or "keep your grip on that life eternal to which you have been called...., Phillips.) But pride undermines whatever progress we make in our spiritual journey, not least if we dare to boast about attaining Christian perfection.[6]

Paul makes clear what sanctifying grace can accomplish in a Christian's life. Perhaps in order to avoid misguided arrogance, he puts it in the form of hope and a prayer:

> I pray that out of his glorious riches he may strengthen you with power through his Spirit in your inner being, so that Christ may dwell in your hearts through faith. and I pray that you, being rooted and established in love, may have power, together with all the Lord's holy people, to grasp how wide and long and high and deep is the love of Christ, and to know this love that surpasses knowledge - that you may be filled to the measure of all the fullness of God.[7]

The reason this passage is so meaningful in this context is its pervasiveness of love and love's giftedness in Christ, at the very same time Paul gives us an incredibly lofty picture of the destiny he wants so badly for his readers.

> To be filled with God is a great thing; to be filled with the fulness of God is still greater; to be filled with all the fullness of God is greatest of all. This utterly bewilders the sense and confounds the understanding, by leading at once to consider the immensity of God, the infinitude of his attributes, and the absolute perfection of each!
>
> ...
>
> By the "fulness of God," we are to understand all the gifts and

[6] Adam Clarke, *Entire Sanctification*, 9.)

[7] Ephesians 3:16-19, NIV.

graces which he has promised to bestow on man in order to his full salvation here, and his being prepared for the enjoyment of glory hereafter. To be filled with all the fulness of God is to have the heart emptied of and cleansed from all sin and defilement, and filled with humility, meekness, gentleness, goodness,justice, holiness, mercy, and truth, and love to God and man. ... A fullness of humility precludes all pride; of meekness, precludes anger; of gentleness, all ferocity; of goodness, all evil; of justice, all injustice; of holiness, all sin; of mercy, all unkindness and revenge; of truth, all falsity and dissimulation; and where God is loved with all the heart, soul, mind, and strength, there is no room for enmity or hatred to him, or to anything connected with him....[8]

Clarke leaves no room for compromise here, and no doubt as to the thoroughness of his vision. Nothing less than a full replacement of our moral and spiritual character will bring about God's new creation. Here he echoes the contrast between the fruit of the Spirit and "the acts of the flesh" in Galatians (Galatians 5: 19-23 NIV) and the opposing lists in Colossians of things that should be "put to death" and other with which we should "clothe []ourselves." (Colossians 3:5-17, NIV) The lists in Colossian appear in a similar context to Clarke's, the perspective of eternity. Thus Paul says: "Since, then, you have been raised with Christ, set your hearts on things above, where Christ is, seated at the right hand of God. Set your minds on things above, not on earthly things. For you died, and your life is now hidden with Christ in God. When Christ, who is your life, appears, then you also will appear with him in glory. (Colossians 3:1-4, NIV)

As with Clarke, in Colossians, heaven is a present, as well as a future reality, one that has a bearing on this life and with which we can and should interact. Heaven is more than a far off goal and not at all like the fantasies of popular imagination. It is a goal and destiny, but already at the center of life for those who seek and enter it. "The kingdom of God is in your midst." (Luke 17:21,NIV; or "The kingdom of God is within you" NKJV.)

Clarke never tries to minimize the power of sin, or to magnify humanity's ability to overcome it. Instead, while he takes the

---

[8] Adam Clarke, *Entire Sanctification*, 19-20.

power of sin very seriously, he emphasizes even more the victorious power of grace: "However inveterate the disease of sin may be, the grace of the Lord Jesus can finally cure it."[9]

Sanctification is much more than a transaction that cancels a debt or waives its penalty, though it does accomplish both. Rather, it offers what the hymn writer Augustus Toplady called "the double cure" for the human condition of sin:

> Be of sin the double cure;
> save from wrath and make me pure.[10]

Eliminating the negativity of sin is an impressive accomplishment by itself. Imagine life without the evils of war, greed, corruption, and hatred. The world and its leaders have proven incapable of bringing these and countless other examples under control. Yet God's new creation embodies far greater changes. First, Jesus speaks to us not only of eradicating obvious evil, but replacing evil with good, and not just ordinary good, but perfection. Nor does he provide a standard of watered down "perfection," with "wiggle room" to accommodate the excuse that we are, after all, "only human." Instead, he says, "Be perfect, therefore, as your heavenly Father is perfect." (Matthew 5:48, NIV)

> But what does this imply? Why, to be saved from all the power, the guilt, and the contamination of sin. This is only the negative part of salvation, but it has also a positive part; to be made perfect – to be perfect as our Father who is in heaven is perfect, to be filled with the fulness of God, to have Christ dwelling continually in the heart by faith, and to be rooted and grounded in love. This is the state in which man was created; for he was made in the image and likeness of God. And this is the state into which every human soul must be raised who would dwell with God in glory.... (Adam Clarke, *Entire Sanctification*, 28.)

Clarke knew that trying to achieve happiness by means of a selfish, sinful life is always going to fail: "And dost thou not

---

[9] Adam Clarke, *Entire Sanctification*, 27.

[10] Augustus M. Toplady, "Rock of Ages, Cleft for Me," The United Methodist Hymnal, Nashville, TN: Abingdon, 1989, #361, v. 1

know that holiness and happiness are as inseparable as sin and misery?"[11]

The last chapters of Revelation show on a cosmic scale the final defeat and elimination of all forms of evil, and evil's radical replacement by God's eternity. There is great cause for rejoicing in the "new heaven" and "new earth" because of this replacement, which will do away with everything that has plagued humanity: "He will wipe away every tear from their eyes. There will be no more death or mourning or crying or pain, for the old order of things has passed away." All these things will vanish as God "make[s] everything new." (Revelation 21: 4-5, NIV) This longed for "new Jerusalem" (Revelation 21:2, NIV) which will answer so much lamentation and hope is built on a foundation of sanctification. It is a city whose citizens arrive prepared.

John Wesley said as much in one his sermons on Jesus' Sermon on the Mount:

"Happy are the poor in spirit; for theirs is the kingdom of heaven."

> This is the kingdom of heaven or of God which is "within" us, even "righteousness and peace, and joy in the Holy Ghost." And what is righteousness but the life of God in the soul, the mind which was in Christ Jesus, the image of God stamped upon the heart, now renewed after the likeness of him that created it? What is it but the love of God because he first loved us, and the love of all mankind for his sake?[12]

The kind of spirit described here is nothing less than the fruit of the Spirit, growing within a willing soul, driving out all contrary impulses, and multiplied across heaven's citizenry.

This same new Jerusalem sparkles "with a brilliance like that of a very precious jewel" because "nothing impure will ever enter it." (Revelation 21:11; 27, NIV) Were anything impure to enter its gates, it would spell the end of the joy and gladness of the city's inhabitants by reducing the reign and glory of the King.

---

[11] Adam Clarke, *Christian Theology*, 207.

[12] Kenneth J. Collins and Jason E. Vickers, eds. *The Sermons of John Wesley: A Collection for the Christian Journey*. Nashville: Abingdon,2013, 481.)

An even more audacious assertion is that the result of God's sanctification project is that his people should "participate in the divine nature."[13]

> We must be made partakers of the divine nature.
>
> God is ever ready, by the power of the Spirit, to carry us forward to every degree of life, light, and love, necessary to prepare us for an eternal weight of glory. There can be little difficulty in attaining the end of our faith, the salvation of our souls from all sin, if God carry us forward to it....[14]

This is the only reason such an audacious claim can be credibly made.

Clarke also points out that, far from the misconception that Christian faith makes for unhappiness in its practitioners, in fact the opposite is the case.

> The soul was made for God, and can never be united to him, nor be happy, till saved from sin. He who is saved from his sin, and united to God, possesses the utmost felicity that the human soul can enjoy, either in this or the coming world.
>
> Our souls can never be truly happy till our wills be entirely subjected to, and become one with, the will of God.[15]

Why would this be? Since God is love (I John 4:8, NIV), the closer we get to him, and to those we love through and because of him, the more we discover and inhabit our true identity and the more we live in an atmosphere of loving interactions, instead of self-seeking ones. To draw near to God means discovering and living out our God-given purpose in life. We stop the forces within ourselves and our world that alienate us from ourselves and each other, and we stop living the shallow, essentially meaningless existence that passes for life. The person set free from sin is "more happy, more useful in the world, and bring[s] more glory to his heavenly Father." Conformity to the pattern of life that we see in Christ means being surrounded with the very best that exists in

---

[13] II Peter 1:4, NIV.

[14] Adam Clarke. *Entire Sanctification,* 30-31.)

[15] Adam Clarke, *Entire Sanctification*, 36-37.

the universe, even as we are liberated from "the corruption in the world caused by evil desires." (II Peter 1:4, NIV) From this God-centered perspective, an awful lot of what the world considers "fun" looks pretty insignificant and often rather shabby.[16]

Clarke put great emphasis on receiving the blessing of entire sanctification "now," with no delay and no halfway measures. He defines "now" as any moment where inspiration and conscience combine to press the need and the promise to form an opportunity. "Whenever, therefore, such blessings are offered, they may be received. ... In the same moment in which he is commanded to turn, in that moment, in that moment he may and should return."[17]

"We are changed from being merely dust and ashes to having the seeds of immortality and incorruptibility. We are made ... 'partakers of the divine nature.'"[18]

If Clarke was emphatic about entire sanctification, it is clear that John Wesley was equally so. In the final days of his life in 1790, John Wesley said to Adam Clarke that retaining the sanctifying grace of God "should be strongly and explicitly urged on all who have tasted of perfect love. If we can prove that any of our Local Preachers or Leaders, either directly or indirectly, speak against it, let him be a Local Preacher or Leader no longer. I doubt whether he should continue in the society. Because he that could speak thus in our congregations cannot be an honest man."[19]

---

[16] Adam Clarke, *Entire Sanctification*, 43.

[17] Adam Clarke, *Entire Sanctification,* 46.

[18] (Ortiz & Keating, *Nicene Creed,* 198.)

[19] *The Works of John Wesley,* ed. Thomas Jackson, 104 (Peabody, Massachusetts: Hendrickson Publishes, Inc., 1984), 13:104, "Letter to Adam Clarke, Nov. 26, 1790."

Chapter 3

Adam Clarke on Eternity

"Very truly I tell you, the one who believes has eternal life."[1]

"Our blessed Lord recapitulates here, what he had said in the preceding discourse. The person who is saved is 1. drawn by the Father: 2. hears his instructions: 3. accepts the salvation offered: 4. is given to Christ Jesus, that he may be justified by faith: 5. is nourished by the bread of life: 6. perseveres in the faith: 7. is not lost, but is raised up on the last day: and 8. is made a partaker of eternal life."[2]

We mortals live in a world of time and limits. The two combine to form lifespans. Psalm 90 famously puts it this way:

> Our lives last seventy years or,
> if we are strong, eighty years.
> Even the best of them are struggle and sorrow;
> indeed, they pass quickly and we fly away.

Thankfully, the same psalm begins with a more balanced picture which at least begins from an eternal perspective:

> Before the mountains were born;
> before you gave birth to the earth and the world,
> from eternity to eternity, you are God.

But then we are plunged back into the depths with these distressing words:

---

[1] John 6:47, NIV)

[2] Adam Clarke, *Commentary*, III: 566.)

You return mankind to the dust...
You end their lives; they sleep.
They are like grass that grows in the morning
– in the morning it sprouts and grows;
by evening it withers and dries up.[3]

Ecclesiastes looks at old age with symbolism and a bit of humor when it speaks of "the day when the keepers of the house tremble, and the strong men are bent, and the grinders cease because they are few, and those who look through the windows are dimmed (Ecclesiastes 12:3, ESV) The new era of dental implants may be providing new "grinders," but the point remains. To a younger person, such talk about aging might seem to have little relevance, but that conclusion could well prove to be shortsighted.

Since the Book of Psalms includes prayers for nearly every situation, from praise and thanksgiving to vengeance and cries for help, it should not surprise us to find this one that deals with old age within an entire spectrum of age related concerns:

For you have been my hope, Sovereign Lord,
my confidence since my youth.
From birth I have relied on you;
you brought me forth from my mother's womb.
I will ever praise you. ...
Do not cast me away when I am old;
do not forsake me when my strength is gone. ...
even when I am old and gray,
do not forsake me, my God.[4]

A very positive reflection on aging is Psalm 92, a portion of which reads:

You have made me as strong as a wild ox;
you have blessed me with happiness
the righteous will flourish like palm trees;
they will grow like the cedars of Lebanon.
They are like trees planted in the house of the Lord,
that flourish in the Temple of our God,
that still bear fruit in old age

[3] Psalm 90:10; 1-6, CSB.
[4] Psalm 71: 5-6; 9; 18, NIV.

and are always green and strong.[5]

Isaiah 46:4 offers a reassuring promise, which reads like a response to Psalms 90 and 71:

> Even to your old age and gray hairs
> I am he, I am he who will sustain you
> I have made you and I will carry you;
> I will sustain you and I will rescue you.[6]

Proverbs 16:31 takes a positive view of old age – "Gray hair is a crown of glory," (Proverbs 16:31, NIV) Leviticus calls Israel to "show respect to the elderly," (Leviticus 19:32, NIV) and another Proverb tells us, 'good people will be remembered as a blessing,(Proverbs 10:7, ESV) but none of these offers the hope of eternity. While there are inklings in the Old Testament, only the New Testament speaks clearly and unambiguously about eternal life and resurrection as the gateway. It is on this foundation that Adam Clarke built his theology of eternity and infinity.

Given Clarke's accomplishments and commitment as a Biblical scholar, it will come as no surprise that Scripture was his first and highest authority as he considered God's eternal, infinite reality and kingdom. Everything he wrote on the subject he either found directly in Scripture or reasonably inferred from Scripture. This is critically important if we are to receive his teachings as more than mere opinions.

At the same time, the subjects he addresses are of such universal magnitude and such great personal significance, that they require and deserve much more than speculation, even from such a wise and learned teacher. The ideas in this chapter are drawn from Clarke's *Christian Theology*, especially, though not exclusively his chapter on heaven.[7]

We most often think of eternity and eternal life as a gift we hope to receive at an indeterminate future time, following death and consequent departure from this life. The Bible reflects this

---

[5] Psalm 92:10; 12-14, GNT.

[6] Isaiah 46:4, NIV.

[7] Samuel Dunn, ed. *Adam Clarke. Christian Theology*. New York, NY: G. Lane & P.P. Sandford, 1842.

same timing, but goes well beyond it. In I John, for instance, eternal life is embodied as Jesus Christ: 'the eternal life which was with the Father and was made manifest to us." (I John 1:2, ESV) This is, of course, the same Jesus identified in John's Gospel as "the way and the truth and the life." (John 14:6, NIV) The point in both readings is that Jesus is more than the bearer of life, or eternal life, but has that life within himself and is himself that light. Thus I John can also say, "This is the testimony, that God gave us eternal life, and this life is in his Son." (I John 5:11, ESV)

Jesus had no intention of keeping eternal life to himself. Instead, he said, "I give them eternal life, and they shall never perish...."(John 10:28) This eternal life has always been the essential nature of God. There has never been a time when God was not, or when he was essentially different from what he revealed himself to be in Scripture. Adam Clarke takes us back to the time when he revealed himself to Moses:

> What is most interesting is [among all the divine attributes] the name by which God was pleased to make himself known to Moses and the Israelites, a name by which the supreme Being was afterward known among the wisest inhabitants of the earth; he who is and who WILL BE what he is. This is a proper characteristic of divine Being, who is, properly speaking, the only BEING, because he is independent and eternal; whereas, all other beings, in whatsoever forms they may appear, are derived, finite, changeable, and liable to destruction, decay, and even to annihilation. When God, therefore, announced himself to Moses by this name [I am], he proclaimed his own eternity and immateriality.
>
> ...
>
> All time is as nothing before him, because in the presence as in the nature of God all is eternity; therefore nothing is long, nothing short, before him; no lapse of ages impairs his purposes, nor need he wait to find convenience to execute those purposes. And when the longest period has passed by, it is as a moment or indivisible point in comparison of eternity.[8]

---

[8] Adam Clarke, *Christian Theology*, 69-70.

Psalm 90 expresses this theme beautifully in words fittingly attributed to Moses: "before the mountains were brought forth, or ever you had formed the earth and the world, from everlasting to everlasting you are God." (Psalm 90:2, ESV) Also closely related is this New Testament passage: "Do not forget this one thing, dear friends: with the Lord a day is like a thousand years, and a thousand years are like a day. (II Peter 3;8, NIV)

Clarke is fascinated with the limitlessness of God, his infinity, so different from the normal experience of humanity, for we are constantly bumping up against our own limitations and those of our world. Here he focuses the limitlessness of Gods attributes:

> The nature of God is illimitable, and all the attributes of that nature infinitely glorious: they cannot be lessened by the transgressions of his creatures, nor can they be increased by the uninterrupted, eternal obedience, and increasing hallelujas, of all the intelligent creatures that people the whole vortex of nature.
>
> This Jehovah is a Being of such infinite perfections, that no defect in him can be imagined; nor can we conceive any thing that might raise, improve, or exalt his nature. Because he is an infinite fullness, nothing can be added: and because he fills all space -the heavens and the earth, and inhabits eternity - nothing can be taken away from him. Whatever exists must necessarily be his creature, or an effect produced by him, the supreme First Cause. As he is independent and self-sufficient, he needs nothing that he has made.[9]

For Clarke referring to God in superlatives is a woefully inadequate beginning. He points to that which cannot be described, so that somehow his audience can see what cannot be seen; to imagine that which Is beyond imagination. "He is not eternity, nor infinity: but he is eternal and infinite. He is not duration, nor space; but he endures always, is present everywhere...." Likewise with eternity:

> Eternity! how can I form any conception of thee? In thee there is no order, no bounds, no substance, no progression, no change, no present, no past, no future. It is an indescribable something,

[9] A. Clarke, *Christian Theology*, 66.

to which there is no analogy in the compass of creation. It is infinity and incomprehensibility to all finite beings.[10]

[10] A. Clarke, *Christian Theology*, 66; 370.

Chapter 4

Adam Clarke on Death and Judgment

"For the wages of sin is death, but the gift of God is eternal life in Christ Jesus our Lord."[1]

"A sinner goes to hell because he deserves it; a righteous man goes to heaven, because Christ has died for him: and communicated that grace by which his sin is pardoned and his soul made holy.[2]

When it comes to the link between death and hell, Clarke leaves no room for equivocation. If "the wages of sin is death," then everyone alive earns death, leading to a very undesirable eternity. "Every man, since the fall, has not only been liable to death, but has deserved it, as all have forfeited their lives because of sin." Harsh - even misanthropic - as this may come across, it simply restates Romans 6:23 and extends another well-known verse from Romans: "all have sinned and fall short of the glory of God."[3]

"It was sin that not only introduced death, but has armed him with all his destroying force. The goad or dagger of death is sin; by this both body and soul are slain." Clark points out the fear that ungodly people have of death is rooted in or exacerbated by

[1] Romans 6:23, NIV.

[2] Adam Clarke, *Commentary*, 4:83.

[3] Romans 6:23, NIV; Clarke, *Christian Theology*, 368; Romans 3:23, NIV.

fear of what follows death. Rather than fearing death while living selfishly, we should live for God the kind of unselfish lives he produces and rewards.

Death is not an opportunity to sort things out, unless we take warning in advance and earnestly give our lives to the Lord. "Death refines nothing, purifies nothing, kills no sin, helps to no glory. Let thy continual bent and inclination be to God, to holiness, to charity, to mercy, and to heaven; then, fall when thou mayest, thou wilt fall well." The trajectory we establish now, and maintain to the end, always by grace with our willing cooperation, will carry us through to a glorious destiny: "the one who endures to the end will be saved." Therefore, "acquire a heavenly disposition while here; for there will be no change after this life."[4]

Clarke points to a mystery, noted by the apostle Paul and noticed by many, which is that some people grow and flourish spiritually even as they decline and weaken physically: It is a good antidote against the fear of death, to find, as the body grows old and decays, the soul grows young and is invigorated. "Therefore we do not lose heart. Though outwardly we are wasting away, yet inwardly we are being renewed day by day." (II Corinthians 4:16, NIV) thus we never need to lose our reason to hope, since the same Lord who fills our days with the riches of his grace stands ready to meet us with an even greater abundance in the next phase of eternity.

> The nearer a faithful soul comes to the verge of eternity, the more the light and influence of heaven are poured out upon it; time and life are fast sinking away into the shades of death and darkness; and the effulgence of the dawning glory of the eternal world is beg1inning to illustrate the blessed state of the genuine Christian, and to render clear and intelligible those counsels of God, partly displayed in various inextricable providences, and partly revealed and seen as through a glass darkly in his own sacred word. Unutterable glories now begin to burst forth; pains, afflictions, persecutions, wants, distresses, sickness, and death, in any or all of its forms, are exhibited as the way to the kingdom, and as having in the order of God an ineffable glory for their

[4] Clarke, *Christian Theology*, 368; Matthew 24:13, ESV.

> result. Here are the wisdom, power, and mercy of God. Here the patience, perseverance, and glory of the saints! Reader, are not the earth and its concerns lost in the effulgence of this glory?[5]

We may be able to imagine the last judgment, only because we have witnessed analogous, lesser judgments, either in person or at a great distance, perhaps on television. We can possibly imagine the setting, and the emotions of some of the participants in the legal drama. If we allow ourselves, we will surely be horrified at the conditions that await condemned prisoners. What we cannot imagine is a trial in which everyone in the courtroom, except the judge, is guilty; where there is no missing, incomplete, or inaccurate evidence, and where the judge is thoroughly aware of all the relevant facts in the case. One additional ingredient that distinguishes this final judgment scene from all the others is that no one stands safely outside the courtroom; no one having coffee and conversation in the hall; no one safely ensconced in front of a screen and out of range of the eventual verdict. Then there is the strangest difference of all: there before the judge is a public defender holding a long list of his clients' names. For some reason, every person on that list; everyone who has a special connection with this one attorney, is transported from the courtroom and set free.

It seems that there is a special relationship between the judge and this public defender that explains this strange courtroom behavior: Prior to the trial, the judge announced his desire that all the defendants should be set free. The judge sent his special emissary, who was now the public defender, to deliver his message to every defendant. Each defendant had to express sincere remorse for their wrongdoings, request a pardon, and put their complete faith in the public defender. And so it worked out. Out of gratitude, the newly freed prisoners began a process of transformation that resulted in a great increase in their happiness and well-being. Those who refused the offer of freedom lost everything, including the freedom they might have enjoyed.

---

[5] Adam Clarke, *Christian Theology*, 369.

Adam Clarke told the eventual spiritual outcome of the salvation story briefly and profoundly, in this way:

> The justice of God is as much concerned in the resurrection of the dead, as either his power or mercy. To be freed from earthly encumbrances, earthly passions, bodily infirmities, sickness, and death; to be brought into a state of conscious existence, with a refined body, and a sublime soul, both immortal, and both ineffably happy - how glorious the privilege![6]

The picture of the transition between worlds at death is vividly drawn by hundreds of Methodists who have experienced and witnessed it, their stories gathered and published by Ohio circuit rider Maxwell Gaddis.[7] In many of these stories we have bright, inspiring portrayals of the passing of faithful people from this life to the next, so that it is almost possible for us to make the journey with them. Often they described growing light around them. Many expressed wonder and surprise at what they were experiencing, as if it were radically different from what they had expected. They were excited about all this and anxious to share their unexpected joy with those around them and others farther away. Many saw their deathbed experiences as confirmation of what they had preached all their lives. In today's skeptical and death denying culture, such accounts may be met with disbelief and explained away, but other responses are possible and conducive to hope.

---

[6] Adam Clarke, *Christian Theology*, 371.

[7] Maxwell Pierson Gaddis. *Last Words and Old-Time Memories*. New York, NY & Pittsburgh, PA: Phillips & Hunt; Cincinnati & Chicago: Walden & Stowe, 1880.

Chapter 5

Adam Clarke on Hell or Negative Eternity

"There was a rich man who was dressed in purple and fine linen and lived in luxury every day. At his gate was laid a beggar named Lazarus, covered with sores and longing to eat what fell from the rich man's table. Even the dogs came and licked his sores.

The time came when the beggar died and the angels carried him to Abraham's side. The rich man also died and was buried. In Hades, where he was in torment, he looked up and saw Abraham, and Lazarus by his side. So he called to him, 'Father Abraham, have pity on me and send Lazarus to dip the tip of his finger in water and cool my tongue, because I am in agony in this fire.'

But Abraham replied, 'Son, remember that in your lifetime you received your good things, while Lazarus received bad things, but now he is comforted here and you are in agony. And besides all this, between us and you a great chasm has been set in place, so that those who want to go from here to you cannot, nor can anyone cross over from there to us.'"[1]

"He sees Lazarus clothed with glory and immortality – this is the first circumstance of his punishment. What a contrast! what a desire does he feel to resemble him, and what rage and despair because he is not like him! We may safely conclude, that the view which damned souls have in the gulf of perdition, of the happiness of the blessed, and the conviction that they themselves might have eternally enjoyed this felicity, from which, through their own fault, they are eternally

[1] Luke 16:19-26, NIV.

> **excluded, will form no mean part of the punishment of the lost.**[2]

While most of this study is devoted to Clarke's positive vision of eternity, there is, as in Scripture, also a negative side: the eternity of hell. As Jerry Walls and C.S. Lewis have argued, the existence of free will requires the possibility that some will choose either to live apart from God or to respond with indifference or neglect to his offer of salvation. "...no human spirit shall ever be found there, but through its own fault. He who refuses the only means of salvation is lost. God willeth not his death. ... He who does not deserve it shall never fall into the bitter pains of eternal death."[3] By "deserve" he means that a person who lands in hell has freely chosen the path that ends there. In fact, it is God's will that everyone should be saved; to enjoy the blessings of heaven and be spared the pains of hell: "God wants all people to be saved and to come to a knowledge of the truth."[4]

Arrival at the destination of heaven is neither automatic nor universal, not even universally desired, difficult as that is to believe or accept.[5] Here is one of Clarke's observations, which includes a reference to the idea of purgatory offering a possible second chance:

> In time and life [there being no room in his thinking for a time, place, or process of purgatory] the great business relative to eternity is to be transacted. On passing the limits of time, we enter into eternity: this is the unchangeable state.[6]

---

[2] Adam Clarke, *Commentary*, III: 464.

[3] A. Clarke, *Christian Theology*, 372.

[4] I Timothy 2:4, NIV.

[5] Jerry Walls. *Hell: The Logic of Damnation*. Notre Dame, IN: University of Notre Dame Press,1992; C.S. Lewis, *The Great Divorce*. San Francisco, CA: HarperOne, 2001.

[6] Adam Clarke, *Christian Theology*, 375; Jerry Walls. *Purgatory: The Logic of Total Transformation*. New York, NY: Oxford University, 2011; Walls. *Heaven, Hell, and Purgatory: Rethinking the Things that Matter Most*. Grand Rapids, MI: Brazos, 2015.

What he describes is a cosmos of mutually exclusive mirror opposites where exquisite joy and excruciating misery exist side by side in unresolved and unresolvable tension forever.

Once again, Clarke draws a horrific line, extending into an endless future: "The torments which a soul endures in the hell of fire will form, for all eternity, a continual, present source of indescribable wo." Then he indulges, as in Dante's Inferno, in speculation as to "various degrees of punishment in hell," and whence they come: "There are various degrees of punishment in hell, answerable to various degrees of guilt; and the contempt manifested to, and the abuse made of, the preaching of the gospel, will rank semi-infidel Christians in the highest list of transgressors, and purchase them the hottest hell!" (A. Clarke, Christian Theology, 374.) God's vengeance against "semi-infidel Christians," those who actually oppose the faith they otherwise profess, is especially fierce.

Clarke sees it as his duty to issue a strong warning to all who still have an opportunity to repent and be saved: "Thy day is far spent, the night is at hand, the graves are ready for thee, and here thou hast no abiding city. A month, a week, a day, an hour, yea even a moment, may send thee into eternity. And if thou die in thy sins, where God is thou shalt never come."[7] There remains hope for those who hear and respond to Jesus' invitation, but only prior to death. Part of his warning is his picture of undying regret the inhabitants of hell experience, knowing they could have chosen otherwise and realizing the harm their choices have caused others. Added to these and similar regrets is the impossibility of accessing any kind of remedy. He goes to great lengths to argue the point that there is no hope of abatement or improvement in this situation; no release for repentance or for lessons learned under any circumstance whatever.[8]

A clear New Testament source for Clarke's ideas here is the parable of the rich man and Lazarus in Luke 16:19-31. In that parable there is a conversation between a rich man who is enduring hell's torment, and Father Abraham, who is an authoritative fig-

---

[7] A. Clarke, *Christian Theology*, 207.

[8] A. Clarke, *Christian Theology*, 373-376.

ure in heaven. The rich man is seeking the aid of one of heaven's residents in moderating the pain he is suffering. There is a particularly poignant irony in the fact that the rich man is begging Father Abraham to secure the relief he is after with the help of a beggar to whom he had shown no compassion when they both were in this life. Father Abraham explains why no aid would be forthcoming:

> Son, remember that in your lifetime you received your good things, while Lazarus received bad things, but now he is comforted here and you are in agony. And besides all this, between us and you a great chasm has been set in place, so that those who want to go from here to you cannot, nor can anyone cross over from there to us.[9]

Nothing the rich man can say would change this ironclad chasm. Even if Lazarus wanted to show undeserved compassion to the rich man, there was no possibility that would allow him to cross the "great chasm [that] has been set in place." One can even wonder whether Lazarus would have been aware of the rich man's appeal.

Against this argument is one that is based on God's everlasting love and compassion. The idea is that God has shown himself, in this life, to champion second chances and spiritual growth. He is well aware of the limitations of our human nature, "for he knows how we are formed, he remembers that we are dust. The life of mortals is like grass, they flourish like a flower of the field." Therefore "he does not treat us as our sins deserve or repay us according to our iniquities." In fact, "The Lord is compassionate and gracious, slow to anger, abounding in love."[10] Why wouldn't that compassion extend to those capable of receiving and benefitting from it in a place where deception is no longer a factor in driving people away from the truth?

Then we have the mysterious passage in I Peter about the gospel being preached to the dead: "For this is the reason the gospel was preached even to those who are now dead, so that they might

[9] Luke 16; 25-26, NIV.

[10] Psalm 103: 14-15; 10; 8, NIV.

be judged according to human standards in regard to the body, but live according to God in regard to the spirit. (I Peter 4:6, NIV) This could refer specifically to Old Testament people who in their lifetimes had no opportunity to respond to Jesus, but could it not just as well apply to people of every generation who lacked that same opportunity, or who could legitimately be blessed by a second chance?

Many, including Adam Clarke, would not accept this reasoning, or this interpretation of Scripture, but surely a case could be made that is faithful to the Bible and consistent with the character of God. In regard to the question of purgatory, for instance, or some kind of experience of purgation that would complete the process of sanctification: would it not better recognize the reality of the human situation than to expect Christian perfection as a universal state of readiness for heaven at the point of death? This would leave the necessity of free will intact and provide for development in each person's relationship to God. The same grace-empowered synergy would drive the movement within and toward holiness as in this life. The goal would still be to "fit us for heaven to live with thee there."[11]

Clarke also pleaded with his fellow preachers to take their role in the rescue mission of Christ very seriously:

> When in the pulpit, be always solemn; say nothing to make your congregation laugh. Remember you are speaking for eternity; and trifling is inconsistent with such awful subjects as the great God, the agony and death of Christ, the torments of hell, and the blessedness of heaven.[12]

As I read Clarke on hell, I find myself acknowledging his relentless effort to be true to Scripture and sensing a lack of compassion for those in the depths of suffering. There is so much horsepower in his words that at times it feels as though Clarke is sitting in the judgment seat, executing vengeance on God's behalf and relishing the opportunity. This is particularly noticeable in

---

[11] John Thomas McFarland. "Away in a Manger," *Our Great Redeemer's Praise*. Franklin, TN: Seedbed, 2023, #197, v. 3.

[12] A. Clarke, *Christian Theology*, 324.

his dealing with purgatory. At the same time, he is completely sincere in trying to warn sinners of impending doom by pointing to the often unforeseen detours and distractions that threaten to lure us from the path of life. Yet I see the error or exaggeration in my initial response to Clarke's "judgment" as I read these words of Samuel Dunn, who knew him well:

> From censoriousness he was perfectly free. His judgment of his brethren was never harsh or severe. He was always ready to speak in their praise and to put the best construction on their sayings and doings. His humility was deep and unaffected. With all his learning there was no parade.

Rather than standing in angry judgment over hopeless sufferers, he was, as when addressing other topics, doing his best to convey a difficult but important Biblical point: "No minister ever lived, who gave a greater prominence in his discourses to the vital truths of Christianity, or who contended for them with more consistency and zeal."

"Consistency and zeal" go a long way toward providing a satisfactory explanation for the harsh tone of some of his words about hell. It is also important to see how heaven and full salvation form the overarching context and compelling contrast to the admittedly dismal description of hell. It is also true that "'the illimitable mercy of Heaven,' the universal redemption of mankind, and especially the witness of the Spirit to the fact of the believer's adoption into the family of God, and Christian perfection, were his favorite topics, those on which he laid the greatest stress...." [13] Clarke does criticize heavily the Catholic teaching and rationale on purgatory as an invention lacking in Scriptural warrant: "A purgatory was feigned by the papists, for the refinement and cleansing of offenses which had not been duly satisfied for in this life..."

As he also says in his commentary on the rich man and Lazarus, the situation of condemned sinners in hell is without hope or remedy. They are irreversibly, "eternally excluded."

---

[13] Samuel Dunn, Biographical Introduction, Adam Clarke. *Christian Theology*. New York, NY: G. Lane & P.P. Sandford, 1842, 34-35; 40.

> We may safely conclude that the view which damned souls have in the gulf of perdition, of the happiness of the blessed, and the conviction that they themselves might have eternally enjoyed this felicity, from which, through their own fault, they are eternally excluded, will form no mean part of the punishment of the lost.[14]

This is the first in his catalogue of sufferings experienced by the residents of hell, the rehearsal of which is frightening, as well as painful. Another sample of these will convey the tone of the whole.

> Even in hell a damned spirit must abhor the evil by which he is tormented and desire the good which would free him from his torment. If a lost soul could be reconciled to its torment, and to its situation, then, of course, its punishment must cease to be such. An eternal desire to escape from evil, and an eternal desire to be united to the supreme good, the gratification of which is forever impossible, must make a second circumstance in the misery of the lost.

Thus, in Clarke's view, even a clear recognition of the difference between good and evil, along with the desire for good and the revulsion toward evil, is not enough to change or reverse the condemnation once in place. Again there is no room for any form of purgatory that might recognize growth or lead to redemption.[15]

Finally, Clarke concludes his chapter on hell in a way that leaves no doubt or vagueness about his major points or about the relentless fate of those condemned to live the negative side of eternity:

> We have no evidence from Scripture or reason that there are any emendatory punishments in the eternal world. The state of probation certainly extends only to the ultimate term of human life. We have no evidence, either from Scripture or reason, that it extends to another state. There is not only a deep silence on this in the divine records, but there are the most positive declarations against it. In time and life, the great business relative to eternity is to be transacted. On passing the limits of time, we enter into eternity: this is the unchangeable state. In that awful and indescrib-

---

[14] Adam Clarke, *Christian Theology*, 373; Commentary, III: 464.

[15] A. Clarke, *Christian Theology*, 373-374.

> able infinitude of incomprehensible duration, we read of but two places or states, heaven and hell; glory and misery; endless suffering and endless enjoyment. In these two places or states, we read of but two descriptions of human beings: the saved and the lost; between whom there is that immeasurable gulf, over which no one can pass. In the one state we read of no sin, no imperfection, no curse: there all tears are for ever wiped away from off all faces; and the righteous shine like the sun in the kingdom of their Father. In the other we read of nothing but "weeping, wailing, gnashing of teeth;" of the worm that dieth not; and of "the fire which is not quenched." Here the effects and consequences of sin appear in all their colourings.... Here no dispensation of grace is published; no offers of mercy made: the unholy are unholy still, nor can the circumstances of their case afford any means by which their state can be meliorated.[16]

Clarke expressed a similar viewpoint in a letter to a Mrs. Wilkinson in 1831. Like John Wesley he maintained an ambitious correspondence on theological and church-related concerns:

> Dear Mrs. Wilkinson, That your friend is gone safe you have no reason to doubt: he who takes Christ in his heart out of time into the eternal world is sure to meet Christ there!
>
> In the various places in my comment, wherever I found a scripture that had been twisted by the universal Restitutionists, I took it out of their hands and freed it from their abuse. A more untenable and deceptive tenet has never been promulgated under the sacred name of religion. Were I seriously to attribute two tenets to the great deceiver, it would be these -1st. there is no devil. 2ndly. The never dying worm will die, and the unquenchable fire will be quenched. By the first all circumspection and watchfulness, &c. are precluded; for why watch against an enemy which does not exist? And by the second all fear of punishment is taken away, and with it the justice of God, the sinfulness of sin, and the atonement of Jesus Christ; for if the fire of hell be inly emendatory, the very idea of punishment is destroyed; and as to the sacrificial offering for sin, it is totally unnecessary, because this is proposed to be done by the infernal flame! But O what an awful risk does that man run in reference to his immortal soul who trusts to a

---

[16] Adam Clarke, *Christian Theology*, 375.

> doctrine supported by a puny, ill-defended, and baseless criticism in matters which concern his eternal salvation or perdition: but the other opinion is already registered, and will not be refuted while the pillars of the everlasting hills endure. As I cannot go into argumentations on the subject at present, I can recommend to your friend a tract by the Rev. Daniel Isaac, which I believe will afford complete satisfaction.
>
> With love to all your family, and prayers for the eternal welfare of the whole, I am yours affectionately, Adam Clarke.[17]

No fear can be envisioned among those in heaven, and no hope for those in hell. For the latter there is only unrelieved suffering, while for the former there is unrestrained joy and celebration. There is no injustice in any of this, nor any possibility of release from the consequences of sin. Whatever second chances might have been available or whatever mercy might have been extended, ended at the moment of death. The picture is grim indeed for the residents of hell, yet can heaven be perfectly happy if its inhabitants are aware of the endless torment going on in the realm of negative eternity? One might also enquire why the repentance so universally necessary and beneficial in this life should have no place in the world to come. Would not the same spiritual dynamics apply?

Yet, for Clarke, and, he would argue, for Scripture, this life offers ample opportunities to accept the generous offer of salvation and its attendant heavenward transformation. Perhaps extending the availability for repentance and sanctification indefinitely would encourage the same selfish neglect and spiritual laziness that constitutes the response of many to the proclamation of the Gospel already.

---

[17] J.B.B. Clarke, e., *Adam Clarke,* 138-139.

Chapter 6

Adam Clarke on Heaven or Positive Eternity

"After this I looked, and there before me was a great multitude that no one could count, from every nation, tribe, people and language, standing before the throne and before the Lamb. They were wearing white robes and were holding palm branches in their hands. And they cried out in a loud voice:

> **"Salvation belongs to our God,**
> **who sits on the throne, and to the Lamb."**
>
> **All the angels were standing around the throne and around the elders and the four living creatures. They fell down on their faces before the throne and worshiped God, saying,**
> **"Amen!**
> **Praise and glory**
> **and wisdom and thanks and honor**
> **and power and strength**
> **be to our God for ever and ever.**
> **Amen!"[1]**

"A great multitude – This appears to mean the church of Christ among the Gentiles, for it was different from that collected from the twelve tribes; and it is here said to be of all nations, kindreds, people, and tongues.

"Clothed with white robes – As emblems of innocence and purity. With palms in their hands in token of victory gained

---

[1] Revelation 7:9-12, NIV.

> **over the world, the devil, and the flesh."**[2]
>
> **"Lord, to whom shall we go? You have the words of eternal life, and we have believed and have come to know, that you are the Holy One of God." (John 6:68-69, ESV)**

"You make known to me the path of life; you will fill me with joy in your presence, with eternal pleasures at your right hand."(Psalm 16:11, *NIV)*, This verse from the Psalms can serve as the interpretive principle underlying much of what Adam Clarke had to say about heaven. Together with Scriptures dealing with glory, kingdom, light, and eternal life, it helps us envision that which is far beyond our imagination. All of his reflection on this subject was guided by the Spirit of truth promised by Jesus: "But when he, the Spirit of truth, comes, he will guide you into all the truth. He will not speak on his own; he will speak only what he hears, and he will tell you what is yet to come." (John 16:13, NIV) It is the Holy Spirit who guided Clarke, whether through the Scriptures or in a more direct manner.

> "Pleasures for evermore," onwardly, Perpetually, continually... an eternal progression. Think of duration in the most extended and unlimited manner, and there is still more; more to be suffered in hell, and more to be enjoyed in heaven. Great God! Grant that my readers may have this beatific sight! this eternal progression in unadulterated, unchangeable, and unlimited happiness."[3]

The overall picture he paints is one of endless spiritual growth, learning, improvement, and enjoyment, continuing the process begun in this life, but uncomplicated by any residual sin in the self or its environment. There will be a pattern of spiritual progress like that described in II Corinthians, "from one degree of glory to another." (II Corinthians 3:18, ESV) Hope will be infinite as one beautiful horizon yields to another. No reason remains for

---

[2] Adam Clarke, *Commentary*, IV: 1017.

[3] A. Clarke, *Christian Theology*, 380.

fear or anxiety since all possible causes for these will have vanished. No boredom is possible, because the one who makes all things new will continue renewing his kingdom. All sorrow will be healed so completely that it will be lost in praise and rejoicing. All good things of this world will be perfected and expanded so that nothing of value or importance will be lost. Ideas that have captured human imagination and admiration will grow in luster as any negative implications associated with them fall to oblivion and the ability to appreciate and extend these ideas will increase dramatically. "Every created intellectual nature is capable of eternal improvement."[4] Pleasure will never again be sullied with selfishness or caught up with pain. Heaven will be a continual, abundant source of every kind of blessing. From heaven's fountains shall flow an endless supply of good things:

> By these perpetual fountains we are to understand endless sources of comfort and happiness, which Jesus Christ will open out of his own infinite plenitude to all glorified souls. These eternal living fountains will make an infinite variety in the enjoyments of the blessed. There will be no sameness, and consequently no cloying with the perpetual enjoyment of the same things; every moment will open a new source of pleasure, instruction, and improvement; they shall make an eternal progression into the fulness of God. And as God is infinite, so his attributes are infinite; and throughout infinity more and more of these attributes will be discovered; and the discovery of each will be a new fountain or source of pleasure and enjoyment. These sources must be opening through all eternity; and yet, through all eternity, there will still remain, in the absolute perfections of the Godhead, an infinity of them to be opened! This is one of the finest images in the Bible.[5]

The passage from Revelation at the beginning of this chapter is part of John of Patmos' vision of heaven, a vision with which Adam Clarke was very familiar. It carries forward the identity of the Church as the people ("all nations," Matthew 28:19, NIV) to whom Christ sent his apostles in his Great Commission, now

---

[4] A. Clarke, *Christian Theology,* 137.

[5] A.Clarke, *Christian Theology*, 379.

gathered in worship around the altar of heaven. The prominence of worship in this passage and throughout Revelation ties together the central ministry of the Church on earth with the central activity of the heavenly kingdom. The main theme of this worship is praise, which is a natural response of God's creatures encountering their Creator face to face. The universal body gathered there as one suggests the earliest vision of Methodism, which incorporated an unlikely assemblage of free and slave, rich and poor, indigenous and European. Here we even have the picture expanded to include angels and other "living creatures," who had been there all along, though generally unrecognized.

Clarke points to the symbols in the reading that describe the spiritual situation and characteristics of the great multitude worshiping in heaven: the white robes representing purity, and "the palms in their hands in token of victory gained over the world, the devil, and the flesh." In these he recognizes the connection between heaven and holiness and the eternal implications of victorious living. All of this is part of the glorious celebration of worship in heaven.[6]

But the best part of the experience of heaven is being in the immediate, incomparable presence of heaven's Lord. Finally,

> It is therefore not heaven merely; it is not the place where no ill can enter, and where pure and spiritual good is eternally present; it is not merely a state of endless blessedness in the regions of glory; it is GOD HIMSELF; God in his plenitude of glories;-God who by the eternal communications of his glories, meets every wish and satisfies every desire of a deathless and imperishable spirit, which he has created for himself, and of which himself is the only portion.

If it were possible to separate heaven from God, as if someone could have one without the other, clearly God, as the Source of all that is good and true, worthy and beautiful, would take precedence over all creation – even his heavenly creation.

> To a soul composed of infinite desires, what would the place or state called heaven be, if God were not there? God, then, is the

---

[6] Adam Clarke, *Commentary*, IV: 1017.

portion of the soul, and the only portion with which its infinite powers can be satisfied.

> It is not heaven they are to inherit, it is God, who is infinitely greater and more glorious than heaven itself. With such powers has God created the soul of man that nothing less than himself can be a sufficient and satisfactory portion for the mind of this most astonishing creature.

Worship in heaven both continues and far exceeds that which began on earth. Even the most beautiful music, or the most discerning sermon, offered up from sincere hearts in sanctuaries built to honor God, can only begin to approach the worship John witnessed around God's throne.

> The song of praise to God, through Christ, begun on earth and protracted through all the generations of men, till the end of time, shall be continued in heaven by those who, having here received the salvation of God, and continued faithful unto death, in the resurrection of the just are taken to that ineffable glory, where, being like him, they "shall see him as he is;" and being raised to his right hand, have fullness of joy and pleasures for evermore: in which state, eras, limits , and periods are absorbed in one eternal duration.[7]

Even before the full realization of what heaven holds, a dawning of glorious light gives an indication of what lies ahead:

> The nearer a faithful soul comes to the verge of eternity, the more the light and influence of heaven are poured out upon it: time and life are fast sinking away into the shades of death and darkness; and the effulgence of the dawning glory of the eternal world is beginning to illustrate the blessed state of the genuine Christian, ... unutterable glories now begin to burst forth; pains, afflictions, persecutions, wants, distresses, sickness, and death, in any or all of its forms, are exhibited as the way to the kingdom... Here the wisdom, power, and mercy of God. Here the patience, perseverance, and glory of the saints! Reader. Are not the earth and its concerns lost in the effulgence of this glory? (A. Clarke, Christian Theology, 369.)

---

[7] Adam Clarke, Christian Theology, 376-378; I John 3:2.

How can finite creatures like ourselves even recognize a description or vision of heaven? Clarke reasons in this way: "The state of eternal glory implies three things: - 1. An absence of all suffering, pain, sin, and evil. 2. The presence of all good, both of the purest and most exalted kind. And, 3. The complete satisfaction of all the desires of the soul."[8]

What role, then does hope play in a situation like this, where evil has already been conquered and relegated to the irretrievable past, and where every cause of suffering has been eradicated? Hope remains and intensifies because God is continually revealing new sources of and reasons for unexpected joy.

> Faith and hope will as necessarily enter into eternal glory as love will. The perfections of God are absolute in their nature, infinite in their number, and eternal in their duration. However high, glorious, and sublime the soul may be in that eternal state, it will ever, in respect to God, be limited in its powers, and must be improved and expanded by the communications of the supreme Being. Hence it will have infinite glories in the nature of God, to apprehend by faith, to anticipate by hope, and enjoy by love.

Even the capacity to grow and enjoy will increase:

> Even in the heaven of heavens, in reference to the infinite and eternal excellences of . God, walk by faith, and not by sight. ... The very nature of the soul shows it to be capable of eternal growth and improvement. ... And is it not this that shall constitute the eternal and progressive happiness of the immortal spirit, namely, knowing, from what it has received, that there is infinitely more to be received...."[9]

Clarke vividly describes the soul's passage from the imperfections of this life to the magnificence of the world to come, even trying to get inside the feelings involved in that transition:

> How wonderful is his lot! A child of corruption, lately a slave of sin and heir of perdition; tossed about with every storm of life; in afflictions many and privations oft; having perhaps scarcely where to lay his head; and at last prostrated by death, and min-

---

[8] A. Clarke, *Christian Theology*, 376-377.

[9] A. Clarke, Christian Theology, 135-136.

> gled with the dust of the earth; but now, how changed! The soul is renewed in glory; the body fashioned after the glorious human nature of Jesus Christ; and both joined together in an indestructible bond, clearer than the indestructible moon, brighter than the sun, and more resplendent than all the heavenly spheres; for having conquered and triumphed in the church militant, it is now set down with Jesus on his throne, as he, having overcome, is set down with the Father on the Father's throne.[10]

His contrasts here are of exquisite beauty and boundless joy! His portrayals of light, clear, bright, and resplendent, are brilliant in the images they elicit and the ambiance they convey. With these the reader is transported into the glorious realm of heaven's reality, compared with elements of earthly existence which the soul is happy to have escaped.

Eternal life is the proper object of an immortal spirit's hope, the only sphere where the human intellect can rest, and be happy in the place and state where God is; where he is seen AS HE IS; and where he can be enjoyed without interruption in an eternal progression of knowledge and beatitude.

Clarke the accomplished Scripture scholar and theologian, consistent with his calling, was drawn to many aspects of heaven, especially those involving the consecrated intellect. He is understandably fascinated with a situation where God, "in an eternal progression," fills and enriches the minds of his people with more and more to enjoy and appreciate learning about and expriencing himself and his new creation. Furthermore, Clarke says that we can go about such pursuits in peace, not frenetically, or competitively, as is so often the case now. In eternity, "the human intellect can rest, and be happy" in God's dazzling, peaceful presence. One can imagine an environment in which knowledge and wisdom are always firmly joined together, and sought only for growth in grace and the sheer enjoyment of learning. The life of the mind in heaven will always center on God "as he is," without being muddied with competing concerns or selfish ambitions of any kind.

---

[10] Adam Clarke, *Christian Theology*, 377.)

> So the truly wise man is but in his twilight here below; but he is in a state of glorious preparation for the realms of everlasting light; till at last, emerging from darkness and the shadow of death, he is ushered into the full blaze of endless felicity.

What an amazing prospect we are shown of a realm where there is "no pain, no misery, no death." The negatives that in this world have such a stranglehold on humanity are completely absent from God's new creation. "From it all evil is absent, and in it all good is present. There the introduction of evil is impossible; and there the loss of good is equally so."

By way of contrast, "An unholy man cannot enter into heaven; and were he in it, it would be no enjoyment to him, because it is not suited to him."[11]

So he concludes his brief, but powerful chapter on heaven by restating the contrasting destinies of people whose lives are consecrated to God with those devoted completely to themselves. He does this in such a way as to attract his readers to one and repel them from the other, since Clarke the scholar is always Clarke the evangelist:

> Think of duration in the most extended and unlimited manner, and there is still more; more to be suffered in hell and more to be enjoyed in heaven. Great God! grant that my readers may have this beatific sight! this eternal progression in unadulterated, unchangeable, and unlimited happiness. Hear this prayer, for his sake who found out the path of life, and who by his blood purchased an entrance into the holiest! Amen and Amen.

---

[11] Adam Clarke, *Christian Theology*, 379.

Chapter 7

An Adam Clarke Miscellany

"God anointed Jesus of Nazareth with the Holy Spirit and power, and ... he went around doing good and healing all who were under the power of the devil, because God was with him."[1]

"Here the apostle refers to Christ as the promised *Messiah*; for as Messiah signifies the *anointed one*, and *Christ* has the same signification in Greek; and the Messiah according to the prophets, and the expectation of the Jews, was to work miracles, Peter proclaims Jesus as the *Messiah*; and refers to the miracles which he wrought, as the proof of it."[2]

+

Adam Clarke was born in Moybeg, County Derry (Londonderry), Ireland, 1760.

+

Some episodes from Adam Clarke's childhood illustrate two points about his eventual orientation to ministry. Both reveal a certain extreme seriousness about sin and repentance. The first point to be taken from these is characteristic of many young Methodist preachers in the early days, whose adult conversion experiences include bitter remorse over not-so serious infractions or typical youthful behavior among their age group - card playing, dancing, disobedience, and general rebelliousness would appear on many of their lists. These fledgling preachers knew how high the standards were for their profession, and they were sure

[1] Acts 10:38, NIV.

[2] Adam Clarke, *Commentary*, 3:776.

they did not measure up, at least not in full, and certainly not in the past. Their parents may have had similar or even harsher standards, leaving these young preachers with either a heavy burden of guilt or a predisposition to identify themselves as serious sinners. The episodes included here from young Adam Clarke's life reveal an extreme sensitivity to sin and punishment, which I imagine ran through the entire family.

> "When but six years old ... One day, as he and another little boy ... sat upon a bank, they entered into conversation on the dreadful nature of eternal punishment. They were so affected with the thoughts that they wept bitterly; and prayed to God to forgive their sins, making mutual promises of amendment. Adam made known his feelings to his mother, and told her that he hoped in future to use no bad words, and always to obey his parents. She was deeply affected, and encouraged him and prayed for him. To her he chiefly owed his early religious knowledge, and even his early religious impressions. It was her practice, especially on the Lord's day, to read to her children, catechize them, and to sing and pray with them.[3]

On one occasion, Adam having disobeyed his mother, she immediately flew to the Bible and opened on Prov. xxx:17, which she read and commented on in the most awful manner:

> The eye that mocketh at his father, and despiseth to obey his mother, the ravens of the valley shall pick it out, and the young eagles shall eat it." He was cut to the heart, thinking the words were immediately sent from heaven! He went out into the field much distressed, and was musing on this terrible denunciation of the divine displeasure, when the hoarse croak of a raven sounded to his conscience an alarm more terrible than the cry of fire at midnight. He looked up, and soon perceived this most ominous bird; and actually supposing it to be the raven ofwhich the text spoke, coming to pick out his eyes, he clapped his hands on them with the utmost speed and trepidation, and ran toward the house as fast as his state of salutary fright and perturbation would permit, that he might escape the impending vengeance![4]

---

[3] Samuel Dunn, *Life of the Author, Adam Clarke. Christian Theology*. New York, NY: G. Lane & P.P. Sandford, 1842. 8-9.

[4] Dunn, *Life*, 9.

[1777- Methodist preachers came to the neighborhood where he lived and he responded to their message.] "His mind became enlightened to see his danger, and he earnestly desired to flee from the wrath to come. His former evil courses were abandoned, his old companions forsaken, and he began to meet in class." [He experienced a typical, though extended Methodist conversion. After a period of anguish,] "he felt a sudden transition from darkness to light."[5]

+

> With this gladness of soul he also received great intellectual enlargement. He could prosecute his literary studies with much greater ease. He now learned more in one day than formerly he was able to do in one month. His mind became enlarged to take in anything useful. He saw that religion was the gate to true learning and science.[6]

+

[Regarding his motivation for ministry:] "The love of God was no sooner shed abroad in his heart, than he felt a yearning pity, a burning charity, for his friends and fellow creatures." [He persuaded his parents to hold morning and evening worship each day in their home, which he generally led. Most of his relatives joined the Methodist society; all came under Methodist influence. He started exhorting and praying with his neighbors in his own and neighboring villages, meeting with widespread acceptance.][7]

+

1782 – Ordeal at Kingswood School and meeting with John Wesley.[8]

+

"Mr. Clarke entered on the regular work of a Methodist travelling preacher, on September 26, 1782, having a tolerable acquaintance with the Scriptures and a heart full of zeal for the salvation of souls;" [and in spite of his inexperience,] "no man despised his

[5] Dunn, *Life*, 9-10.

[6] Dunn, *Life*, 20.

[7] Dunn, *Life*, 11-12.

[8] Wesley Tracy. *When Adam Clarke Preached, People Listened*. Kansas City: Beacon Hill, 1981, 22-24.

youth. ... Souls were awakened, and many young persons especially began earnestly to inquire the way of salvation." [His first] "circuit was very extensive, comprising no less than thirty-one towns and villages, and he had to preach and travel several miles every day, beside attending to various other duties; yet such was his thirst for learning, that he availed himself of every opportunity for cultivating his mind, by rising early, reading on horseback, and 'never whiling away his time.'"[9]

+

"The duties of preaching and pastoring, however thoroughly done, did not keep Adam Clarke from intense study and scholarly achievement. He practiced what he preached concerning good use of time. ... He learned twenty languages.... Biblical studies consumed more study time than anything else. He translated the entire Bible from the original tongues before starting his Commentary.[10]

+

> [Another circuit, this time in Cornwall:] "a very heavy circuit" [required endurance of the elements.]"The places were numerous, and he had to preach almost every week in the year in the open air, and at times too when the rain was pouring down, and when the snow lay deep upon the ground. 'But the prosperity of Methodism made everything pleasant'. A heavenly flame broke out, and great numbers joined the society." [There were those on the circuits who recognized the special gifts and graces he brought to the ministry, especially his learning, eloquence, and dedication to his calling.][11] "All the great range of his studies were pursued in light of God's word and God's call upon his life."[12]

+

[1788 - married Mary Cooke, with this understanding of his commitment to Methodist ministry:]

"As I am at the disposal of Mr. Wesley and the conference, and they can send me whither they please, will you go with me whithersoever I am sent?"

---

[9] Dunn, *Life*, p. 14

[10] Tracy, *Adam Clarke Preached*, 26.

[11] Dunn, *Life*, 15.

[12] Tracy, *Adam Clarke Preached*, 32.

[her reply:] "Yes, if I take you, I take you as a minister of Christ, and shall go with you to the ends of the earth."[13]

+

[1790 - appointed to Dublin, where he established "The Stranger's Friend Society" charity, the first of several such ministries. He also established schools in several communities.][14]

+

> [One who often heard him described Clarke's preaching in glowing terms:] "Brother Clarke is, in my estimation, an extraordinary preacher; and his learning confers great lustre on his talents: he makes it subservient to grace. His discourses are highly evangelical: he never loses sight of Christ. In regard of pardon and holiness, he offers a present salvation. His address is lively, animated, and very encouraging to the seekers of salvation. In respect to the unawakened, it may indeed be said, that he obeys that precept, "Cry aloud; spare not; lift up thy voice like a trumpet." His words flow spontaneously from the heart; his views enlarge as he proceeds; and he brings to the mind a torrent of things new and old. While he is preaching, one can seldom cast an eye on the audience without perceiving a melting unction resting upon them. ... He generally preaches from some part of the lesson for the day; and, on the Sabbath morning, from the gospel for the day: this method confers an abundant variety on his ministry."[15]

+

"Clarke studied widely, processed all things through his own mental mill, and what came forth had his own mark upon it."[16]

+

"'The whole place, to borrow the language of the upper region, seemed celestialized and the atmosphere itself appeared as though it had undergone a kind of chemical process which enabled the audience to breathe of nothing but heaven.'"[17]

+

---

[13] Dunn, *Life*, 16-17.

[14] Dunn, *Life*, 17-18.

[15] Dunn, *Life*, 19-20.

[16] Tracy, *Adam Clarke Preached*, 34.

[17] Tracy, *Adam Clarke Preached*, 35.

"In the typical theological development of a Clarke sermon we have the picture of a perfect God, the utter sinfulness of man, and the presentation of the gracious atonement of Christ and the full salvation it affords through pardon and purity. Each step is proved by logic and Scripture. Then with "earnest affection" he urges the needy to seek God.[18]

+

Clarke was elected President of the British Methodist Conference and literally picked up and carried to the chair [1806]. He eventually served three terms in that prestigious position.[19]

+

[Clarke served in every kind of setting from London & Dublin to Cornwall & the Shetland Islands.

+

"No man in any age of the church was ever known, for so long a period, to have attracted larger audiences.[20]

+

"Clarke thought the genius of the Methodist movement was that there was no stopping place. After conversion a person was called to sanctification, and after that continual growth in order to stay among the redeemed."[21]

+

"Adam Clarke modeled the ideal combination of personal religion and social concern. He shared with Wesley the idea that the Church should change the world on the basis of Christian principles. Clarke was generous to a fault in his personal life, worked incessantly to help others, and also lent his influence and support to the people and organizations which were trying to solve the most crucial concerns."[22]

+

"Among the most vigorous opponents of slavery were the Methodists; and among the Methodists who opposed slavery most vigorously was Adam Clarke."[23]

---

[18] Tracy, *Adam Clarke Preached,* 47.

[19] Dunn, *Life*, 22.

[20] Tracy, *Adam Clarke Preached*, 30.

[21] Tracy, *Adam Clarke Preached*, 118.

[22] Tracy, *Adam Clarke Preached*, 138.

[23] Tracy, *Adam Clarke Preached*, 144.

[In 1831, Dr. Clarke received a letter from William Case, a leader among Methodist missionaries to indigenous people in Canada, introducing Peter Jones, an indigenous Methodist preacher visiting England. This letter indicates Clarke's influence well beyond Britain and Ireland. A portion of this long letter shows the importance of this connection.]

> Although unknown to you personally; yet, through the medium of your excellent writings, I have, on my part, contracted a friendship as strong and endearing as is generally produced by social and brotherly intercourse. Through these, many of my doubts have been removed, my faith strengthened, and my understanding guided; yea, my heart has often been made glad in seeing so clearly unfolded, the immeasurable love of God, and the riches of grace in Christ Jesus. These benefits I have received in common with my younger brethren in the ministry in this province [Upper Canada, now Ontario], and who are now in the providence and grace of God, in some measure, under my care. And I take this opportunity for myself, and for them, to convey to you the gratitude which I know they feel for the helps you have provided toward the right understanding of the pure gospel and the word of God.
>
> The bearer, Mr. Peter Jones, a chief of the Chip-pe-way nation of Indians, is an itinerant minister, and missionary to the tribes of his nation; he is also engaged in translating the Scriptures into the Chip-pe-way tongue: not understanding the Greek, he has derived much help from your Commentary, to which he has continually referred.... As Mr. Jones is desirous of making his acknowledgments personally, I take the liberty of introducing him to you as an humble Christian, and faithful minister of Jesus Christ, respectfully requesting you will afford him such counsel and advice as his youth, inexperience, and situation among strangers, may seem to require.
>
> Brother Jones was among the first converts of the Chip-pe-way station. [Case continues at some length to describe the special contributions Jones had made and his promise as an evangelist. He details all that Jones hopes to accomplish on his travels, including familiarizing himself with the international Church and raising financial support for the missionary work in Canada.][24]

[24] J.B.B. Clarke, ed., *Adam Clarke*, 136-138.

[1832, upon the death of Robert Scott, Clarke wrote:] "Mr. Scott changed mortality for life."[26]

+

Clarke wrote a letter in 1832 to the Missionary Society of the Methodist Episcopal Church in which he declined their invitation for a speaking engagement for reasons of age and diminished strength. In this letter he conveys his perspective on a variety of issues, thus providing what may well have been a synopsis of themes in addresses and sermons he would be unable to deliver in person:

> I am an old man, having gone beyond three-score years and ten, and, consequently, not able to perform the labour of youth. You would naturally expect me to preach much; and this I could not do .... I would say to all, Keep your doctrines and your discipline, not only in your church-books, and in your society-rules, but preach the former without refining on them, observe the latter without bending it to circumstances, or impairing its vigour by frivolous exceptions and partialities. As I believe your nation to be destined to be the mightiest and happiest nation on the globe, so I believe that your church is likely to become the most extensive and pure in the universe. As a church, abide in the Apostles' doctrine and fellowship. As a nation, be firmly united; entertain no petty differences; totally abolish the slave-trade; abhor all offensive wars; never provoke even the puniest state; and never strike the first blow. Encourage agriculture and friendly traffic. Cultivate the sciences and arts; let learning have its proper place, space, and adequate share of esteem and honour. If possible, live in peace with all nations; retain your holy zeal for God's cause and your country's weal; and, that you may ever retain your liberty, avoid, as its bane and ruin, a national debt.[26]

+

"And the treasures of knowledge which his unwearied industry had drawn together, were all made subservient to the more effective execution of his ministerial office."[27]

---

[25] Dunn, *Life*, 27.

[26] Dunn, *Life*, 29. The wisdom of his words have continued to make them highly relevant.

[27] Dunn, *Life*, 34.

> [The evaluation of colleague and biographer, Samuel Dunn:] Dr. Clark's preaching was chiefly expository. He endeavoured to explain the terms in his text; to ascertain the precise meaning of the Holy Ghost; and then to apply to the understandings and consciences of his hearers the hallowing truths thus discovered. His preaching, though argumentative, was decidedly evangelical. No minister ever lived, who gave a greater prominence in his discourses to the vital truths of Christianity, or who contended for them with more consistency and zeal.[28]

+

"Historical study was vital to Clarke. In three of his recorded sermons he tells the people that the Epistles can be properly understood only when we know the 'circumstances of the writers, and the state of the people to whom the letters were addressed.'[29]

+

"His chief work, and on which his name will descend to posterity with the greatest lustre is his 'COMMENTARY ON THE HOLY SCRIPTURES.' It is undoubtedly the most critical and literary, and at the same time the most spiritual and practical, of any work of the kind, that was ever published in any living language."[30] He was "the man who taught the Methodists how to study the Bible" and "preached some 15,000 sermons."[31]

"Clark believed that every preacher should be an ardent student of the Word."[32]

+

"God requires whatever his word requires. He will not bring down the moral law to our weakness and fall; but he will bring us up to it."[33]

+

[28] Dunn, *Life*, 40.

[29] Tracy, *Adam Clarke Preached*, 56.

[30] Dunn, *Life*, 42-43.

[31] Tracy, *Adam Clarke Preached*, 9,12.

[32] Tracy, *Adam Clarke Preached*, 57.

[33] Adam Clarke, in Tracy, *Adam Clarke Preached*, 64.

"He never sought, but rather shunned, literary honours; thinking himself undeserving of them: but learned and literary societies thought otherwise."[34] "In those days it was unheard of for a lowly Methodist preacher to be so widely acclaimed."[35]

[Clarke's response to a colleague's question as to whether he should undertake a particular field of study:] "A Methodist preacher should know everything."[36]

+

"August 26, 1832, he fell asleep in Jesus," in that year's cholera epidemic. His body was laid to rest next to John Wesley at Wesley's City Road Chapel in London.[37]

+

[Written by Adam Clarke shortly before his death:]

The Seasons of Adam Clarke's Life

I have enjoyed the spring of life -
I have endured the toils of its summer -
I have culled the fruits of its autumn,
I am now passing through the rigors of its winter;
And I am neither forsaken of God,
Nor abandoned by man.
I see at no great distance the dawn of a new day,
The first of a spring that shall be eternal.
It is advancing to meet me! I run to embrace it!
Welcome! Welcome! eternal spring! Hallelujah![38]

+

A 45 foot high obelisk honoring Adam Clarke stands at Portrush, County Antrim, Ireland (cover photo.)

---

[34] Dunn, *Life*, 45.
[35] Tracy, *Adam Clarke Preached*, 27.
[36] Dunn, *Life*, 45.
[37] Dunn, *Life*, 42; Tracy, *Adam Clarke Preached*, 9.
[38] Tracy, *Adam Clarke Preached*, 165.

www.ingramcontent.com/pod-product-compliance
Lightning Source LLC
LaVergne TN
LVHW020653100826
845148LV00012B/2460

9781609472191